EXTRA! EXTRA! READ ALL ABOUT IT

by

Greta Barclay Lipson

Bernice N. Greenberg

illustrated by Helen S. Nadler

GOOD APPLE, INC.
BOX 299
CARTHAGE, IL 62321

What's a castle for? — A rhetorical
question at Castle Frieberg. With cherished
memories of an Italian summer, 1980.

TABLE OF CONTENTS

INTRODUCTION

Extra! Extra! — Read All About It! Yes, the emphasis is on read. Because READING is so basic to education and the NEWSPAPER is such an integral part of our society, the two combine to create an effective winning vehicle for instruction.

But let's not stop there! Research reveals that 94 percent of the literate adults in the United States read the newspaper. This public includes an age range of 16 years and older, a broad cross section of men and women, occupations, and levels of education. This profile has existed for the past 50 years.*

Outside of the classroom children are constantly bombarded by the media. Whether we like it or not, whether the curriculum or the teacher's manual provides for it — we are thrust into the media arena. We leave the stands as spectators and suddenly enter the arena as participants in local and world affairs. We are there — on the scene — with the reporter!

Students internalize the news in a deeper dimension when they see it, when they hear it, and when they talk about it. It is then that a full range of learning takes place. Through the use of the newspaper the teacher can motivate students and effectively teach the basic skills.

The newspaper is introduced in this book as an instructional aid, a vehicle for critical and analytical thinking and a resource for curriculum development.

The teacher can use the diversified newspaper activities in this book to prepare a variety of lessons and units for students. The lessons can be changed and/or adapted to different subject areas and grade levels. This book can also

---

*Cited by *Journal of Reading*, Vol. 23, No. 2, Nov. 1979, p. 162, Research: "How We Understand the News," John T. Guthrie. Study conducted by Book Industry Group, May 1978.

become a catalyst for the teacher's own creative ideas and inspiration.

The daily newspaper on your doorstep is among the richest and most available sources for creative thinking.

The newspaper in education is a natural. Schools use books, TV, films, AV tapes and other costly equipment and supplies. But why not welcome the least costly and most versatile information source of all — the newspaper, which is a "living textbook." It opens the door to opinion, debate, drama and fantasy. Not the least of these offerings is the refinement of academic skills.

The newspaper, among its more obvious qualities, recommends itself because it is cheap, expendable, disposable, universal, and malleable. It can be read, discussed, dissected and analyzed. It can be used to swat flies, wrap garbage, make a hat, train your pet, or make a paper-mache dinosaur. Finally, it doesn't weigh too much, it doesn't cost too much and if you lose this "compendium of learning" there is another one available tomorrow!

HOW TO USE THIS BOOK

When we started to write this book we began to read newspapers differently than ever before! No longer were we totally occupied with content for its own sake. It was possible to approach a segment of the newspaper and ask the questions: How many different curriculum areas does this section or article suggest for classroom skills? What style of writing is used in this article? And how does this subject stimulate creative expression?

With these challenges, **Extra! Extra!** assumed its own personality. Two characteristics join the book together. One, the identification of the writing style in each section. And the other is the organization of the book.

Extra! Extra! is divided into 14 major sections with 193 activities. Each section begins with a **CONCEPT PAGE** which provides a conceptual framework for instructional background. This is followed by **NEWS TO USE,** a series of activities which enhance understanding through skill development and creative lessons. Finally, each section ends with the **THE BIG ACTIVITY,** a well developed learning experience that reinforces and heightens the concept. A concluding section, **THE CLASS NEWSPAPER** provides a production guide to your own classroom newspaper. If you do not plan to produce a school newspaper, the activities in this final section can be used as a means of evaluating the information the students have acquired.

The organization of **Extra! Extra!** assumes special importance for the teacher, since it can be adapted as a model in dealing with **any** section or **any** newspaper. Simply provide your own conceptual background and activities.

The invitation to introduce your own curriculum emphasis is implicit in the plan. We invite you to extend the possibilities offered by the book. Once started, there is no limit to the challenge. **Extra! Extra!** suggests only the beginning of your own innovative enterprise.

A LITTLE HISTORY

In working with newspapers it is interesting to note something about the beginnings of the press in America. The first printing press in this country was set up in Cambridge, Massachusetts, in 1638. It was 52 years later on September 25, 1690, that Benjamin Harrison, a former editor of a Whig newspaper in London, England, published the first American newspaper called *Publick Occurrences Both Forreign and Domestick*. It was four pages and measured 6" x 9 1/2". Three of the four pages were for news and one blank page was to be used for a personal letter or whatever pleased the reader.

The plan was to publish the paper "once a month (or if any Glut of Occurrences happen, oftener)." Unfortunately, four days after the paper was published, the governor and the council suppressed it because it included gossip about the King of France and criticism of the government's conduct in the French and Indian War. Thus it was the fate of the first paper published in the American colonies to print only one issue. In those days freedom of the press was yet to become a matter of social concern.

It took 14 years for another newspaper to appear which was called the Boston *News-letter,* founded by John Campbell, the Scottish postmaster of Boston. Happily, the paper lasted for 72 years and was operated by four different owners. This newspaper was followed by the Boston *Gazette* in 1719, edited by William Brooker and printed by James Franklin, the older brother of the famous statesman Benjamin Franklin. As one would expect, Benjamin was the apprentice boy in the print shop. Benjamin followed his brother who later established the New England *Courant.* Had Benjamin been born in modern times he probably would have started as a paper carrier!

The *Courant* was noteworthy in the history of newspapers because its news coverage was clever and lively. It was designed to entertain the townspeople in many ways with the publication of letters, essays and verse. In addition to the news, the importance of the *Courant* was enhanced by the contribution of Ben Franklin's "Dogwood Papers." Young Ben believed that his brother would not accept his humorous feature if he knew the source and so Ben wrote under the pseudonym "Silence Dogwood." Surreptitiously young Ben would slip his copy under the print shop door at night. The editors and readers were delighted with the light, clever writing which was printed every two weeks. When older brother James unmasked the mystery writer, James was less than pleased and abruptly stopped the column. Older brothers could be overbearing even in those days!

Most important, the *Courant* was the first newspaper which spoke out freely without regard for offending the government. But this conduct was not without penalty, for James Franklin was imprisoned for one month because of his political criticism. Despite Franklin's imprisonment, the *Courant* continued to be critical of the ruling powers. The case of Franklin and the subsequent public stir marks the genesis of concern for freedom of the press.

Triumphantly, after the American Revolution, freedom of the press was guaranteed by the Constitution. The First Amendment reads in part: "Congress shall make no law respecting an establishment of religion, or prohibiting the free exercise thereof; of abridging the freedom of speech, or of the press." Americans soon regarded the newspaper as an important source of information and an essential part of life.

By the early 1800's circulation of papers was still low because they were bought by subscription which was very costly — $8 to $10 yearly. This all changed by the middle 1800's when the first cheap newspapers were successfully sold on the streets by the New York *Sun* which peddled the "penny paper" in 1833. Because of significant technological changes, which included the faster steam-driven press, penny papers became possible. The new cheap paper dealt with local and human interest stories and was often sensational. In four months of circulation the New York *Sun* went from 2,000 to 5,000 copies and made a solid profit.

Newsboys appeared on streets for the first time and cheap papers brought news to the common people with resounding success. There was now competition for street sales. Among the new papers at this time was the New York *Tribune,* which was published in 1841 under the guidance of Horace Greeley who is regarded as the father of American journalism. It was he who believed that editors had to take an ethical stand and had an obligation to improve society. When Greeley said, "Go West, young man," it was his advice to the unemployed of New York City.

The next most significant paper which followed was the *New York Times*, first published on September 18, 1851. From its very beginnings it developed a reputation for calm, forceful integrity which it maintains to this day. It was, among other qualities, the first newspaper to emphasize foreign as well as domestic news. It must be noted that the *Times* could not compete for a penny and had to raise its price to 2 cents!

Interestingly, there were several factors which contributed to the flourishing newspaper business. The population was growing; the advent of public education created greater literacy; oil lamps and later gas lamps were replacing candlelight (which made reading easier); and the newspaper had become a cheap and easily available commodity. All of this meant an ever-increasing growth of circulation, along with the strong desire of the American public to know about current national affairs.

The newspaper business prospered and in 1895 the three Scripps brothers established the first chain of newspapers known as the Scripps-McRae League of Newspapers which included four major papers.

Penny papers continued into the 1900's and by 1930 some still sold for 2 pennies. A major criticism, however, was that they carried too much advertising of patent medicines. Of course, the revenues from advertising were one of the factors which enabled the papers to be sold so cheaply.

In our democratic country there has always been a sustained interest in the affairs of the world. The press was and still is the best medium for keeping abreast of the news for all of the people.

A
MODERN
UPDATE

To cast history in a modern light, newspapers are still considered to be the best medium for daily news coverage, the popularity of television notwithstanding.

This country has approximately 1,800 daily newspaper companies and 8,500 weekly newspapers. In an average daily newspaper, about 60 percent of it contains ads while only 40 percent is actually news. Some papers are semiweekly and weekly. More than 60 million copies of newspapers are circulated in one year.

In an address to the National School Boards Association in Miami in 1979, Walter Cronkite stated that 60 percent of the people were not adequately informed about current affairs. He added that it was the job of newspapers to provide the detailed story of the day's events since **all of the spoken words in an average half-hour news broadcast "equal the number of words on two-thirds of the front page of a standard newspaper."**[1]

When we read the newspaper we can scan, reread, stop, or study the material. We can be selective about what we read, picking and choosing according to our own interests. We can read fast or slowly and do just as we please when we read through the newspaper. When we watch news coverage on television, it is on the air and quickly gone. It does not lend itself to examination, analysis or questions. Newspapers, however, can give readers the news both briefly and in depth in the same daily issue.

Modern technology makes it possible to bring the news rapidly and accurately to the reader. In order to compete with radio and TV for quick mass communication, newspapers introduced electronic technology into every phase of its operation. The view of the newspaper business with offices full of typewriters is an outdated notion. Now, journalists in big city newspapers sit at cathode ray tube

[1]*Update:* Newspaper in Education, Vol. 5, No. 8, October 1979, American Newspaper Publishers Association Foundation, The Newspaper Center, Washington, D.C.

terminals (CRTs) to produce their written copy. These TV-type machines have small screens located above the keyboard. The writing appears on the screen as it is typed. These stories are stored in a computer until they are to be edited and then are transmitted electronically to be set into type for the newspaper. Computers produce 2000 words per minute from computerized news items which flow steadily into the news department 24 hours a day.

A modern press can produce a 112-page edition at a rate of 70,000 papers per hour when running at top speed. More than 1,250 gallons of ink are used daily for an average city newspaper.

The single most important component in the production of a newspaper is the people. From the reporters to the news carriers — from ten people on a small town paper to 30,000 on a big city paper — each and every one contributes to the life force of the newspaper.

The purpose of a newspaper is to reach the largest number of people with the most information for the least amount of money. The newspaper depends upon a mass audience and is aimed at anyone who can pay the price of the daily paper. In order to better understand the meaning of a mass audience, let's look at the following facts: The "soaps" on TV have an audience of about 15 million viewers; a championship fight may have 45 million viewers. The daily circulation of a big city newspaper may be 630,000. Interestingly, the *Wall Street Journal* is the largest circulating newspaper in the United States, with a reading audience of 1,599,559 per day as of 1979. This is followed by the *New York Daily News, Los Angeles Times* and *New York Times.*

How does a newspaper reach the largest mass audience possible, considering the many reading abilities of that audience? The criteria for the level of newspaper language is that a sentence must be understood the first time it is read. Reporters must say what they mean and mean what they say. Information must be accurate and precise because a newspaper is in the business of informing the public. Indeed, the newspaper is a **service.** Its purpose is to inform, persuade and entertain.

A SAMPLE OF THE ORGANIZATION OF A METROPOLITAN NEWSPAPER

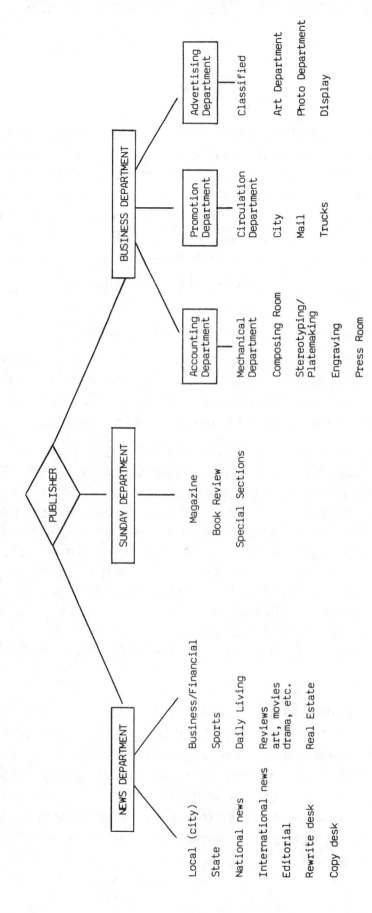

This chart is provided as a general guide and cannot account for rapid changes in technology or individual newspapers.

I. ANATOMY OF THE FRONT PAGE

LAYOUT OF FRONT PAGE

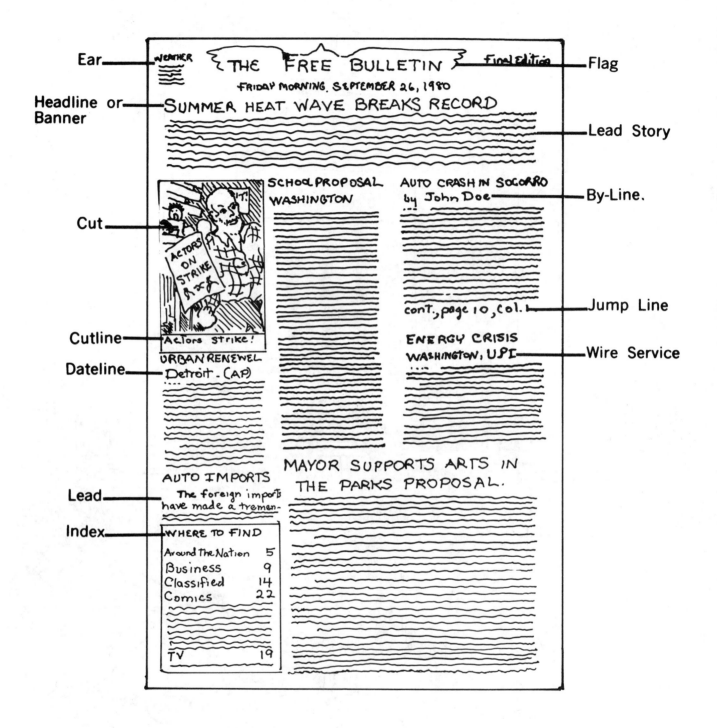

Ear — WEATHER

THE FREE BULLETIN — Flag (Final Edition)

FRIDAY MORNING, SEPTEMBER 26, 1980

Headline or Banner — SUMMER HEAT WAVE BREAKS RECORD

Lead Story

Cut

SCHOOL PROPOSAL
WASHINGTON

AUTO CRASH IN SOCORRO
by John Doe — By-Line

Cutline — Actors Strike!

cont., page 10, Col. 1 — Jump Line

ENERGY CRISIS
WASHINGTON, UPI — Wire Service

Dateline — URBAN RENEWEL Detroit. (AP)

AUTO IMPORTS

Lead — The foreign imports have made a tremen-

MAYOR SUPPORTS ARTS IN THE PARKS PROPOSAL.

Index — WHERE TO FIND

Around The Nation	5
Business	9
Classified	14
Comics	22
TV	19

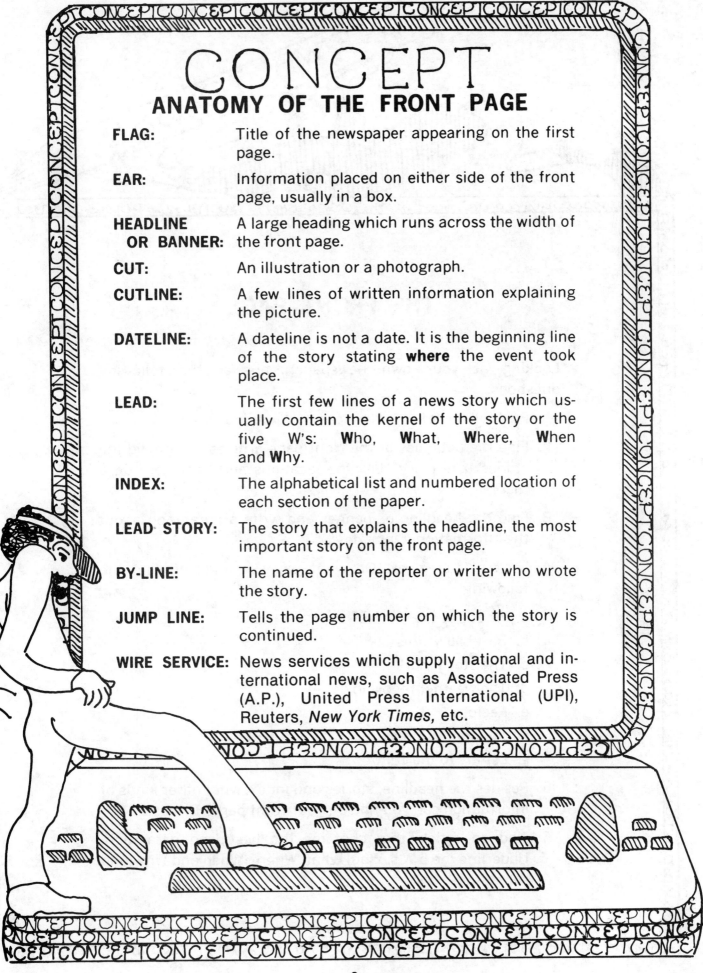

CONCEPT

ANATOMY OF THE FRONT PAGE

FLAG: Title of the newspaper appearing on the first page.

EAR: Information placed on either side of the front page, usually in a box.

HEADLINE OR BANNER: A large heading which runs across the width of the front page.

CUT: An illustration or a photograph.

CUTLINE: A few lines of written information explaining the picture.

DATELINE: A dateline is not a date. It is the beginning line of the story stating **where** the event took place.

LEAD: The first few lines of a news story which usually contain the kernel of the story or the five W's: **W**ho, **W**hat, **W**here, **W**hen and **W**hy.

INDEX: The alphabetical list and numbered location of each section of the paper.

LEAD STORY: The story that explains the headline, the most important story on the front page.

BY-LINE: The name of the reporter or writer who wrote the story.

JUMP LINE: Tells the page number on which the story is continued.

WIRE SERVICE: News services which supply national and international news, such as Associated Press (A.P.), United Press International (UPI), Reuters, *New York Times,* etc.

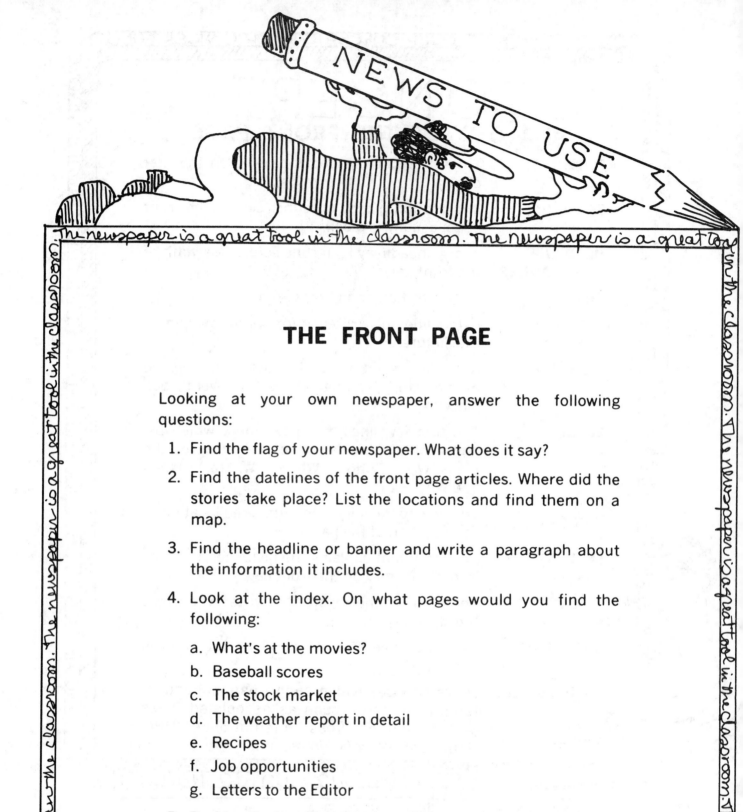

THE FRONT PAGE

Looking at your own newspaper, answer the following questions:

1. Find the flag of your newspaper. What does it say?

2. Find the datelines of the front page articles. Where did the stories take place? List the locations and find them on a map.

3. Find the headline or banner and write a paragraph about the information it includes.

4. Look at the index. On what pages would you find the following:

   a. What's at the movies?
   b. Baseball scores
   c. The stock market
   d. The weather report in detail
   e. Recipes
   f. Job opportunities
   g. Letters to the Editor

5. Besides the headline, stories and index, what other kinds of information can you find on your front page? Discuss.

6. Find an article that contains the best lead paragraph. Underline the 5 W's: **W**ho, **W**hat, **W**here, **W**hen and **W**hy (and sometimes **H**ow).

News to Use

The Princess of Mongoose visits old flame in Toledo.

7. How many personalities are mentioned on the front page? List them and indicate what their jobs are.

8. List the titles of articles and the wire services which supplied the news (AP Associated Press), (UPI United Press International), (Reuters), (TASS).

9. How many writers have a by-line on the front page? Write down their names.

10. Select the cut (photo) on the front page and rewrite the cutline (information under picture).

11. Select a total of 10 words from the headline or in the title of a front page article. Then scramble the letters of each word. Exchange them with a partner. See how many words each of you can figure out. Search for clues on your front page. Put the words spelled correctly on the bottom of the page.

Examples: **Millions** Spent on Roads.
nslioilm
Judge's **Trip** Backfires.
rpti
Midwest Hit By **Tornadoes**
rnotdaeso

HOKEY HEADLINES

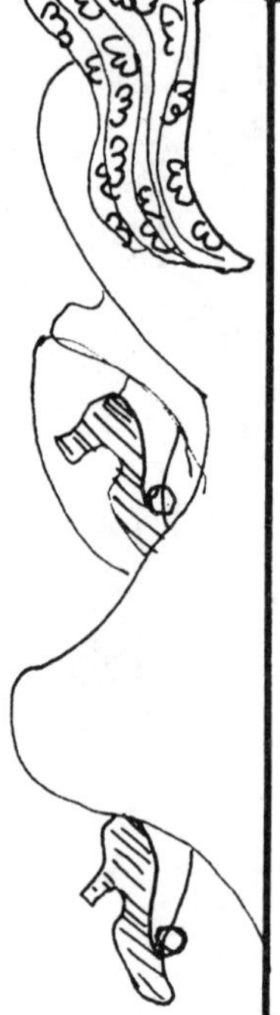

The function of a headline is to summarize the contents of the most important story on the front page. The larger the headline, the more important the story. Some guidelines for writing headlines are:

a. Compress the information.

b. Use the present tense.

c. Use your newspaper as a punctuation guide to capitalize your headline.

d. Use humor and imagination.

e. Don't use articles (the, a, an) or other words which can be omitted.

f. Don't use weak verbs.

Write your own funny headlines from literature, history, modern times or the future. For example:

— Egg Head Goes To Pieces On Wall Street
        (Literature) — (Mother Goose)

— Roman War Stops For Caesar Salad Brunch
        (History)

— Tragedy Shakes Peers Of Two Households
        (Literature) — (Romeo & Juliet)

— Ludwig Hits It Big In A Fit

        (Music)

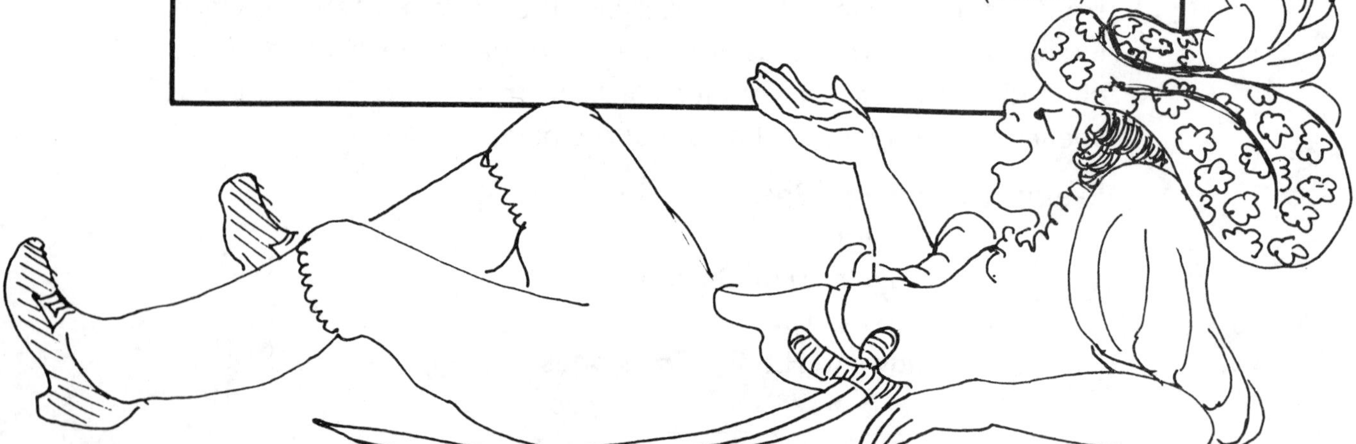

II. A NEWSPAPER STORY

CONCEPT

A NEWSPAPER STORY

A newspaper story may be approached in many ways and with three basic writing styles: informative, persuasive and entertaining. Sometimes a combination of these styles will be used.

A Straight News Story (Informative) deals with the facts and contains the 5 W's: **W**ho, **W**hat, **W**hen, **W**here, **W**hy and sometimes **H**ow. The story usually tells the climax at the beginning. Generally most of the important facts are contained in the first paragraph.

A Human Interest Story (Entertainment) does more than provide the facts. It emphasizes something interesting, funny, sad or unusual about people, animals, places and things, etc.

An Editorial (Persuasive) analyzes and interprets the news. Editorial opinions represent those of the writers on the editorial staff and may be expressed about anything which happens in the news. Editorials must appear on an editorial page. In that way readers understand that an editorial is a viewpoint and not factual, straight news.

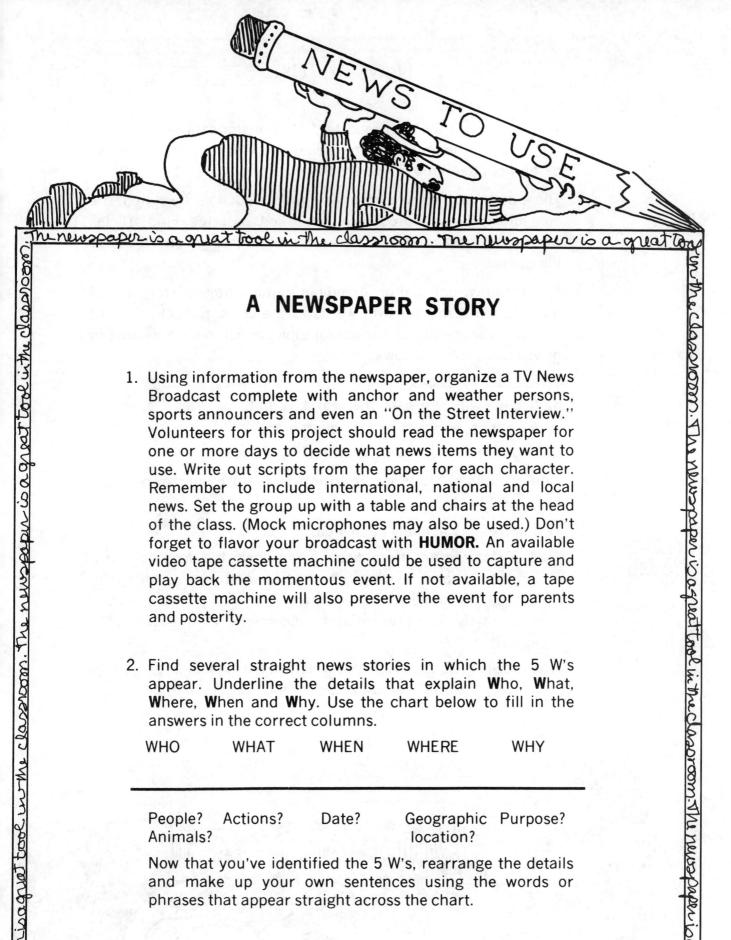

A NEWSPAPER STORY

1. Using information from the newspaper, organize a TV News Broadcast complete with anchor and weather persons, sports announcers and even an "On the Street Interview." Volunteers for this project should read the newspaper for one or more days to decide what news items they want to use. Write out scripts from the paper for each character. Remember to include international, national and local news. Set the group up with a table and chairs at the head of the class. (Mock microphones may also be used.) Don't forget to flavor your broadcast with **HUMOR.** An available video tape cassette machine could be used to capture and play back the momentous event. If not available, a tape cassette machine will also preserve the event for parents and posterity.

2. Find several straight news stories in which the 5 W's appear. Underline the details that explain **W**ho, **W**hat, **W**here, **W**hen and **W**hy. Use the chart below to fill in the answers in the correct columns.

WHO	WHAT	WHEN	WHERE	WHY
People? Animals?	Actions?	Date?	Geographic location?	Purpose?

Now that you've identified the 5 W's, rearrange the details and make up your own sentences using the words or phrases that appear straight across the chart.

News to Use

3. You are an "on the spot reporter" at an historical event. Choose the time in history and the celebrity. Write a straight news paragraph. Remember, you are there!

4. There are many ways to introduce quotes, such as: he stated, she concluded, they shouted, said, remarked, asserted. Find articles which contain quotes and make a list of verbs which introduce the quotes.

5. Find a funny, unusual or incredible human interest story. Cut it out and tell it in your own words to the class. Collect a "Weird File" for storytelling. Some actual topics which have appeared in newspapers are as follows:

   a. A hotel for dogs
   b. A club which insists the world is flat
   c. A robber who fell asleep on the job
   d. A boy who has teeth growing in his feet

6. Find an animal story and rewrite it to feature your own pet or favorite animal.

7. This news story actually happened.

   A 20-foot garden hose disappeared down the deep hole of a neighbor's lawn, leaving 6 feet of hose on the surface. The hose could not be pulled out by any of the neighbors who tried desperately. The firemen and policemen tried unsuccessfully as well.

   Write down a list of possibilities which would explain this mystery. Have everyone offer a solution. Select the best explanation.

News to Use

8. Find a human interest story about a child or a teen-ager in the paper. Tell it in your own words to the class.

9. A businessman in your neighborhood wants to build a parking lot on a playground which he owns. Take a stand and write an editorial convincing your readers that it must be done or should not be done.

10. Who wrote the editorial in today's paper? What was the topic the editor wrote about?

11. Feature articles are given a prominent place in the newspaper. The feature is a story with an angle. It is not strictly news, but is interesting and timely. Choose a partner and read the headlines of feature articles. Make up what you think the feature story was all about. Give a brief oral presentation to the class. Here are some actual examples of feature headlines:

   a. It's too cold for mosquitoes
   b. When it comes to wine they know their onions
   c. The tough choices on energy conservation
   d. Sailing in an ocean storm is better than "Star Wars"
   e. Most older Americans caught in money squeeze
   f. Daisy returns to Royal Oak school for fifth year
   g. Women march for equal rights
   h. Thief steals 5 gallons of ice cream on 100 degree day
   i. Snake makes getaway in church
   j. Kids bike for hospital funds

News to Use

12. Now that you know about the three styles of newspaper writing, look through the **entire** newspaper and find one article that fits into each category below. Then list the title of each article and the subject. Take your time.

INFORMATIVE

For example:

Title of Article: School Marching Band Wins Honors.

Subject of Article: Our own Carson School Band won the first prize in the state competition with ten other schools.

Title of Article:

Subject of Article:

PERSUASIVE

Title of Article:

Subject of Article:

ENTERTAINING

Title of Article:

Subject of Article:

CHOOSE YOUR WRITING STYLE

A news story may be written in one of three styles:

1. **Informational** — as straight news — facts (the five W's: **W**ho, **W**hat, **W**here, **W**hen, and **W**hy).

2. **Persuasive** — as an editorial — personal opinion on any issue.

3. **Entertaining** — as human interest — humorous, sad, interesting stories about people, animals, places or things.

Here is a list of possible topics which can be written in each of the three styles:

a. Beth Loren was accepted on the boys' football team.
b. Man shoots computer
c. Gas rationing introduced
d. Teen-agers form school cleanup squad
e. Mayor recommends Hamburger Haven Restaurant be closed

Choose one of the topics listed above and write a news story in one of the three styles. Triads of students may get together to work with a topic in all the styles suggested. A class reading should follow the assignment to listen to the diversity of results.

Read your stories to the class. Ask them to identify the style as being **human interest** (entertaining) **straight news,** (informational) or **editorial** (persuasive).

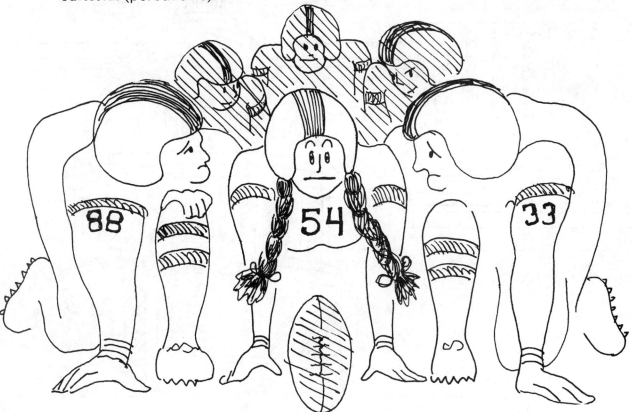

III. NEWS: INTERNATIONAL, NATIONAL, STATE & LOCAL

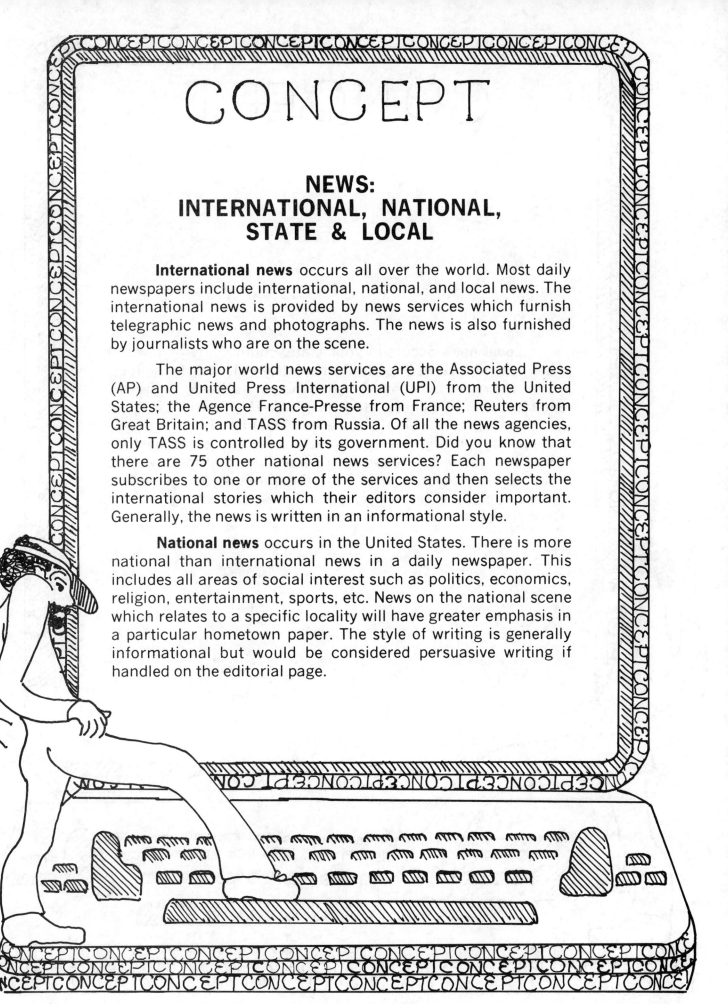

CONCEPT

NEWS: INTERNATIONAL, NATIONAL, STATE & LOCAL

International news occurs all over the world. Most daily newspapers include international, national, and local news. The international news is provided by news services which furnish telegraphic news and photographs. The news is also furnished by journalists who are on the scene.

The major world news services are the Associated Press (AP) and United Press International (UPI) from the United States; the Agence France-Presse from France; Reuters from Great Britain; and TASS from Russia. Of all the news agencies, only TASS is controlled by its government. Did you know that there are 75 other national news services? Each newspaper subscribes to one or more of the services and then selects the international stories which their editors consider important. Generally, the news is written in an informational style.

National news occurs in the United States. There is more national than international news in a daily newspaper. This includes all areas of social interest such as politics, economics, religion, entertainment, sports, etc. News on the national scene which relates to a specific locality will have greater emphasis in a particular hometown paper. The style of writing is generally informational but would be considered persuasive writing if handled on the editorial page.

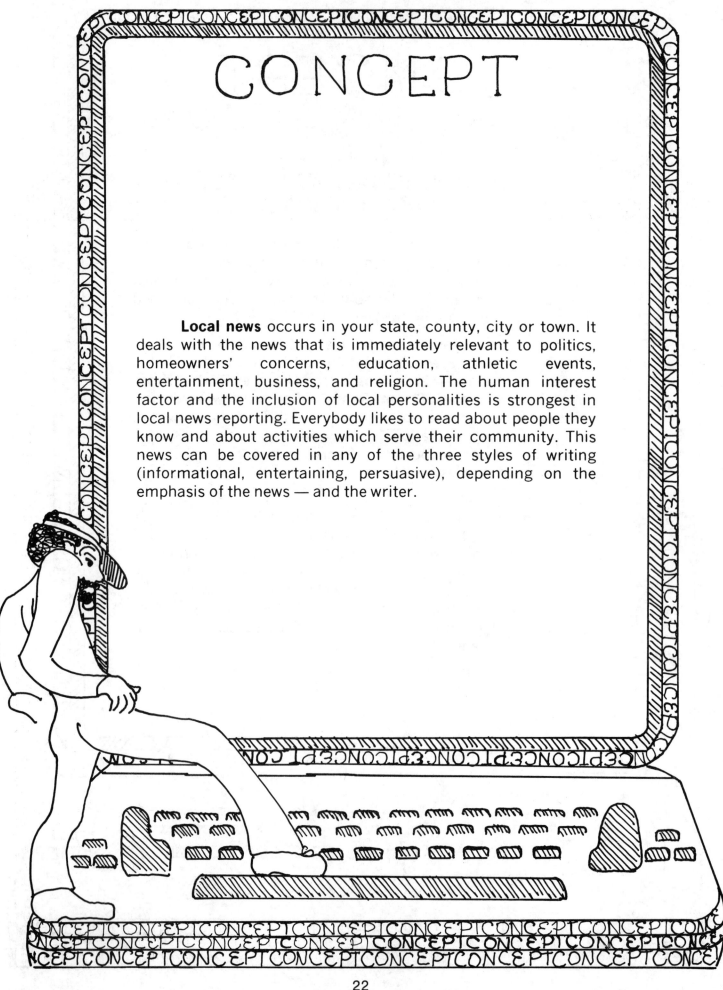

CONCEPT

Local news occurs in your state, county, city or town. It deals with the news that is immediately relevant to politics, homeowners' concerns, education, athletic events, entertainment, business, and religion. The human interest factor and the inclusion of local personalities is strongest in local news reporting. Everybody likes to read about people they know and about activities which serve their community. This news can be covered in any of the three styles of writing (informational, entertaining, persuasive), depending on the emphasis of the news — and the writer.

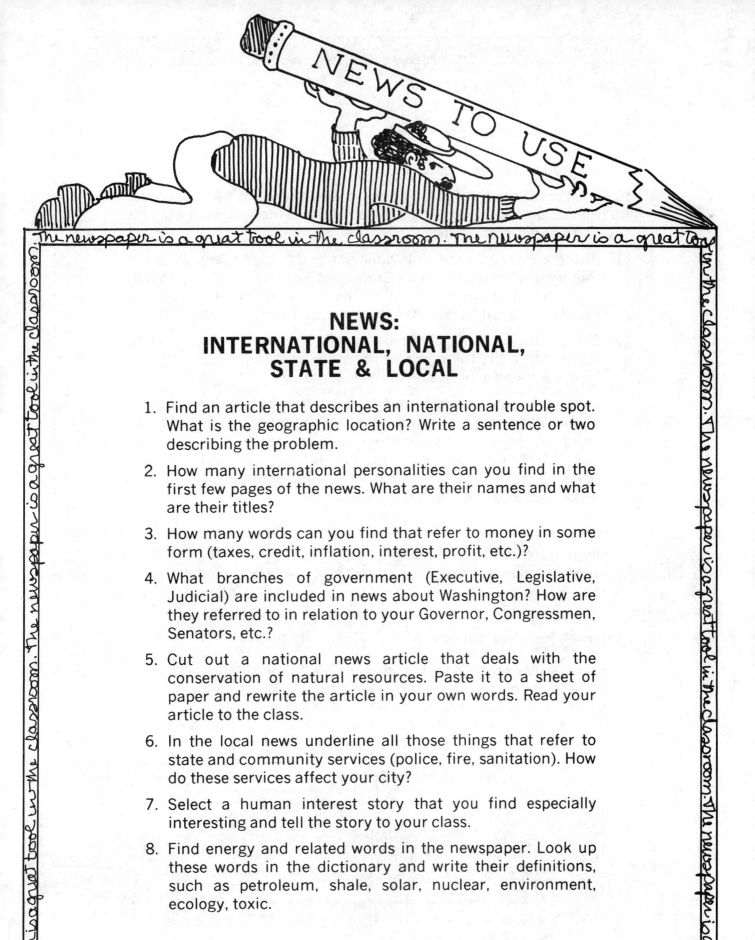

NEWS:
INTERNATIONAL, NATIONAL, STATE & LOCAL

1. Find an article that describes an international trouble spot. What is the geographic location? Write a sentence or two describing the problem.

2. How many international personalities can you find in the first few pages of the news. What are their names and what are their titles?

3. How many words can you find that refer to money in some form (taxes, credit, inflation, interest, profit, etc.)?

4. What branches of government (Executive, Legislative, Judicial) are included in news about Washington? How are they referred to in relation to your Governor, Congressmen, Senators, etc.?

5. Cut out a national news article that deals with the conservation of natural resources. Paste it to a sheet of paper and rewrite the article in your own words. Read your article to the class.

6. In the local news underline all those things that refer to state and community services (police, fire, sanitation). How do these services affect your city?

7. Select a human interest story that you find especially interesting and tell the story to your class.

8. Find energy and related words in the newspaper. Look up these words in the dictionary and write their definitions, such as petroleum, shale, solar, nuclear, environment, ecology, toxic.

News to Use

9. Choose a partner. Each of you list five recreational events in the local news that are of interest. Tell why. Then compare your individual choices with each other.

10. Start a collection of difficult or unusual words in the newspaper that could cause a spelling problem. Define them. Keep a card file of these difficult words.

11. Divide a piece of paper into four parts. Put four headings at the top: International, National, State, and Local. Find the headlines of articles that would fit each of the four classifications. Cut the headlines out and paste them in the proper subject classification.

12. Contact the post office for a listing of the postal abbreviations for states. Write the full name of the state next to the abbreviation. How are states abbreviated in the newspaper?

13. An acronym is formed from the first letters or syllables of other words (Webster). It stands for an organization, agency or company, etc. The following are some common acronyms: FBI, HEW, GOP, IRS. Define them. For fun, put as many of the following acronyms together in one paragraph so that it makes sense. Add some of your own, as you wish!

GM	General Motors	USSR	United Soviet Socialist Republic
FBI	Federal Bureau of Investigation	FTC	Federal Trade Commission
CIA	Central Intelligence Agency	RDA	Recommended Daily Allowance
UN	United Nations	NOW	National Organization of Women
GOP	Grand Old Party	NYC	New York City
IRS	Internal Revenue Service	TWA	Trans-World Airlines

Example: My teacher took a trip on TWA to the USSR, sponsored by NOW. When she came back to NYC, the CIA was waiting to talk to her. They found her at the UN Building where she had arrived in a GM car. She was talking to an agent from the IRS who wanted to know how she could afford such an expensive trip.

EXECUTIVE   LEGISLATIVE   JUDICIAL

THE RIPPLE EFFECT

There is a constant flow of information and interdependence between the international, national and local scene. The news flows both ways and has one or more effects either locally, in the nation or in the world.

For example: **The High Price of Oil from the Mideastern Countries** — This has a direct influence on national policy in Washington, local problems, and the gas price paid by every family in the country that has a car. Draw a picture that demonstrates this fact.

For example: **Volcano erupts in the state of Washington — apple orchards destroyed** — This is an example of how a local event has a direct effect all over the country. Destroyed orchards mean fewer apples will come from Washington. This shortage of production will increase the demand from other apple-producing states like Michigan and New York. Because of the reduced crop, the price will probably increase.

Find a news item, **or make up your own,** which begins in your hometown or state that might have national or international impact. Your event may be related to science, music, art, athletics, education, agriculture, medicine, etc.

CONCEPT

EDITORIAL PAGE

The editorial page is very important. It is here that we find the opinions of the newspaper as stated by the editor. On almost all other pages there is straight news reporting, but the editorial page is a forum for presenting different points of view, analysis and interpretation.

The role of a newspaper in a democratic society is to inform and also state opinions to influence the readers on social and political issues. This is done through the use of **persuasive writing.** This form of writing not only states facts but seeks to convince. The writing is very forceful because of the choice of strong words. The editor or others who express their opinions on this page use special writing techniques which they hope will make the reader see things from their point of view.

The international, national and local matters which editors discuss may affect the lives of all citizens. Editors deal with political, social and economic issues. These may be related to school taxes, voting for political candidates, protecting the rights of children and older people, supporting equal rights for women, the building of a nuclear power plant, the role of business in pollution, or deposits on soda pop bottles. In short, an editorial may discuss any controversial subject on which there are differences of opinion, bias, morality, or vested interests.

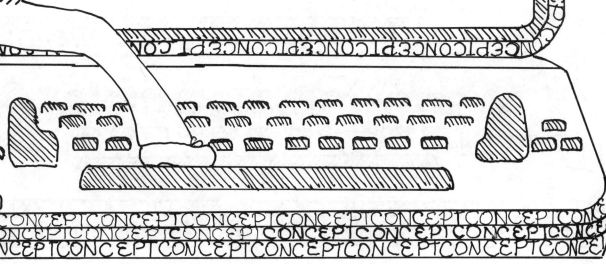

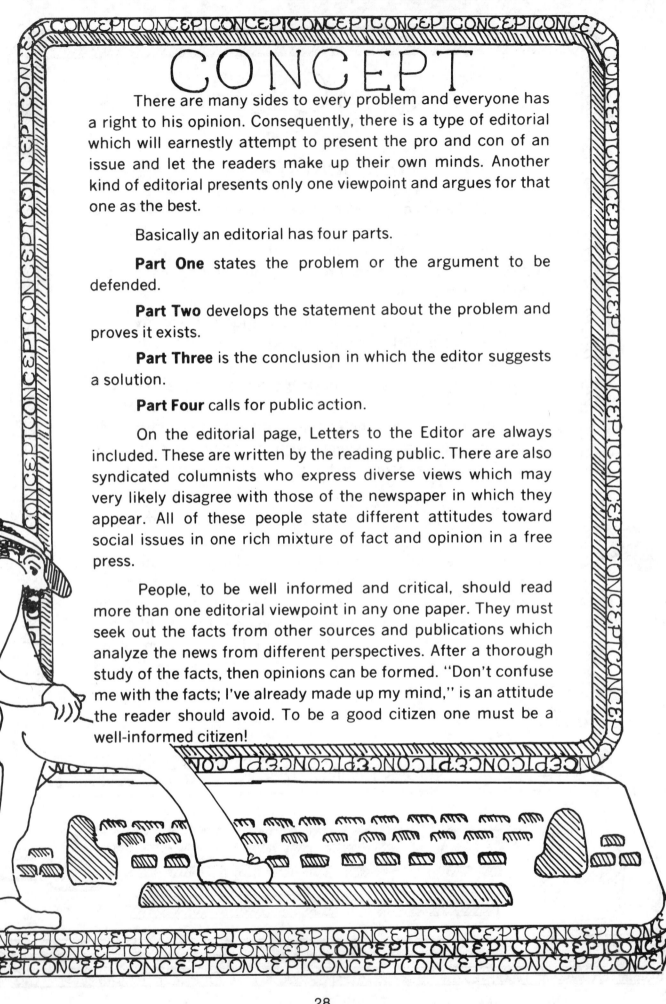

CONCEPT

There are many sides to every problem and everyone has a right to his opinion. Consequently, there is a type of editorial which will earnestly attempt to present the pro and con of an issue and let the readers make up their own minds. Another kind of editorial presents only one viewpoint and argues for that one as the best.

Basically an editorial has four parts.

Part One states the problem or the argument to be defended.

Part Two develops the statement about the problem and proves it exists.

Part Three is the conclusion in which the editor suggests a solution.

Part Four calls for public action.

On the editorial page, Letters to the Editor are always included. These are written by the reading public. There are also syndicated columnists who express diverse views which may very likely disagree with those of the newspaper in which they appear. All of these people state different attitudes toward social issues in one rich mixture of fact and opinion in a free press.

People, to be well informed and critical, should read more than one editorial viewpoint in any one paper. They must seek out the facts from other sources and publications which analyze the news from different perspectives. After a thorough study of the facts, then opinions can be formed. "Don't confuse me with the facts; I've already made up my mind," is an attitude the reader should avoid. To be a good citizen one must be a well-informed citizen!

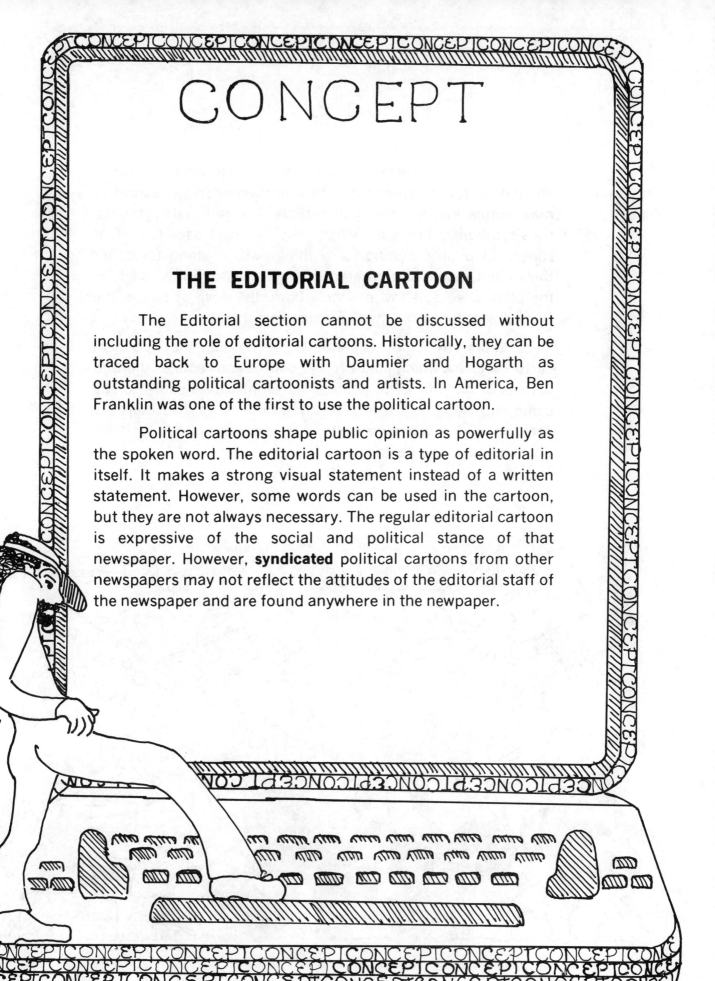

CONCEPT

THE EDITORIAL CARTOON

The Editorial section cannot be discussed without including the role of editorial cartoons. Historically, they can be traced back to Europe with Daumier and Hogarth as outstanding political cartoonists and artists. In America, Ben Franklin was one of the first to use the political cartoon.

Political cartoons shape public opinion as powerfully as the spoken word. The editorial cartoon is a type of editorial in itself. It makes a strong visual statement instead of a written statement. However, some words can be used in the cartoon, but they are not always necessary. The regular editorial cartoon is expressive of the social and political stance of that newspaper. However, **syndicated** political cartoons from other newspapers may not reflect the attitudes of the editorial staff of the newspaper and are found anywhere in the newpaper.

Concept

An editorial cartoon is a simple graphic presentation of an opinion. It is created to inform, entertain or anger readers. It may be mischievous, funny or serious. The editorial cartoonist uses **symbolism** in his drawings, just as a poet uses figures of speech in poetry. Symbols are things which stand for other things and may be interpreted in more than one way, such as the picture we all know of Uncle Sam, the dove of peace, the Democratic donkey or the Republican elephant.

Satire (ridicule) is another technique that political cartoonists use which pokes fun at people and reduces them to objects of laughter. The political cartoonist uses satire to say something serious, but in a funny way. It is hard to consider someone seriously when a cartoonist has drawn him to look like a clown, a pig, or a weasel.

Concept

The cartoonist caricatures real-life people who are in the public eye by taking a facial or body feature and distorting or exaggerating it, such as a mouthful of teeth, a nose like a ski slope or hair like a rat's nest. Caricatures are always recognizable. They attract the attention of the reader and can be embarrassing for public figures. Sometimes people in the public eye enjoy being visible and brought to the attention of the readers despite the cartoonist's caustic pen.

Political cartooning is part of our American history and is a little over 200 years old. It is considered a strong instrument of communication. An effective cartoon has a "punchy" message which is communicated immediately from the cartoonist to the reader. Here, once again, we see evidence of the old adage, "A picture is worth a thousand words."

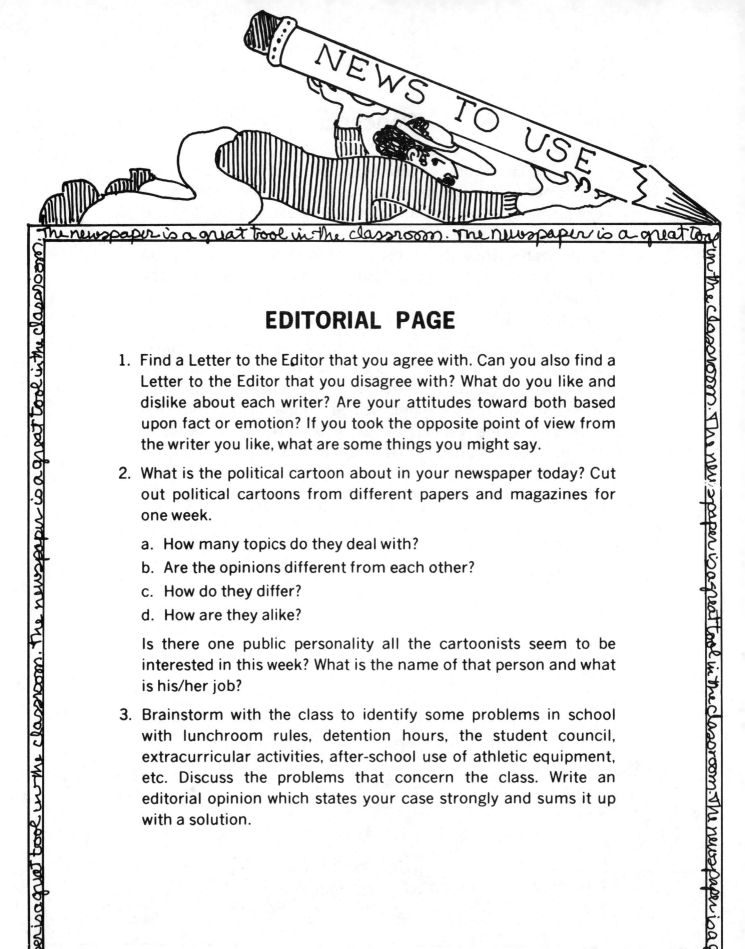

EDITORIAL PAGE

1. Find a Letter to the Editor that you agree with. Can you also find a Letter to the Editor that you disagree with? What do you like and dislike about each writer? Are your attitudes toward both based upon fact or emotion? If you took the opposite point of view from the writer you like, what are some things you might say.

2. What is the political cartoon about in your newspaper today? Cut out political cartoons from different papers and magazines for one week.

   a. How many topics do they deal with?

   b. Are the opinions different from each other?

   c. How do they differ?

   d. How are they alike?

   Is there one public personality all the cartoonists seem to be interested in this week? What is the name of that person and what is his/her job?

3. Brainstorm with the class to identify some problems in school with lunchroom rules, detention hours, the student council, extracurricular activities, after-school use of athletic equipment, etc. Discuss the problems that concern the class. Write an editorial opinion which states your case strongly and sums it up with a solution.

News to Use

4. Write down one or more quotes from Letters to the Editor which you think are unusual or funny statements. Here are two actual examples:

"It is time for young Americans to stop loving and respecting their cars more than their elders."

"Two-thirds of the people in the world go to sleep hungry, while in America, according to the latest figures, we spend an average of $61.81 a year to feed each dog in the USA and $38.06 for each cat. What is this country coming to when we can spend $3.2 billion in an average year for pet food?"

5. Find some subject headings anywhere in the newspaper (**not** just the Editorial section), about which there may be a difference of opinion. The subjects can be unimportant or important. List them and read them to the class. Ask your classmates what they think these various points of view might be. Make sure you have ideas about the possibilities for disagreement on these topics. For example:

City Refuses to Install Traffic Light
Athletic Field Closes on Weekends
Motorcyclists Refuse to Wear Helmets
Group Denied Parade Permit in City
10 p.m. Curfew for Children

6. What are the topic headlines in your Editorial section today? For example: "BIG OIL: FULL SPEED AHEAD, AND DON'T WORRY ABOUT CONSERVING." Write down each headline and compose a one-sentence comment about each.

7. Use the editorial page of your newspaper to identify statements which are facts and others which are opinions. Select one article or Letter to the Editor. Underline **facts** with two red lines. Underline **opinions** with one red line.

8. Cartoons which appear on the editorial page also make very strong social and political statements. Cut out a political cartoon and paste it on a piece of paper. In your own words explain what the cartoonist is trying to say. Can you tell what his/her attitude is about the subject? Does the cartoon poke fun at the subject or shock the reader? Why is ridicule or making fun of something such a strong weapon?

9. Read through the Editorial section of your newspaper. Select an issue to which you have a reaction and write a letter to the editor about it. Before doing so be sure to read the rules as stated in the newspaper about writing such a letter. What are the rules and what are the reasons for them? Why must you include your name and address? For example:

FULL ADDRESS, PLEASE
Letters may be edited or condensed. Shorter ones usually will be given preference. All should be signed originals, with the full address of the writer. Letters that also are sent to other publications usually will not be used. Writers normally should be limited to no more than one letter each 30 days. Names will be withheld only for extraordinary reasons.

News to Use

10. Try to draw your own cartoon which makes a statement about something at home or at school. It can be funny or serious. If you can't draw, try to explain your cartoon plan to someone who can draw it for you.

11. When we look at cartoons, it is obvious that every message we get does not have to be expresssed in words. Look through the entire newspaper for pictures that demonstrate strong emotions for us **instantly** without words. These may be pictures of people or animals which show joy, sorrow, love, friendship, fear, curiosity, etc. Make a booklet with your best collection of these pictures entitled "The Power of Pictures." What is meant by the statement, "A picture is worth a thousand words"?

News to Use

12. Look through the editorial page and find words or phrases which are strong or loaded with emotion. Make a list of these phrases to be read aloud. They may have nothing to do with the facts but may strongly influence a person's opinion. For example:

EMOTIONAL WORDS AND PHRASES

 a. The screams of hysterical voices at the meeting . . .
 b. Our do-nothing mayor will once again give a speech
 c. This plan sounds like a dictator's plot
 d. Taxpayers' good money supports courses at school which are frills
 e. All **good,** patriotic Americans will agree with us
 f. Those loud-mouth kids don't know the meaning of good manners

13. When one thing stands for something else, either visual or in figurative speech, that is **symbolism** (for example: the dove of peace with an olive branch in its beak, Uncle Sam, The Democratic donkey, the Republican elephant, or the Russian bear). Editorial cartoonists use symbolism all the time which is a remarkable skill. What kinds of symbols in political cartoons have you seen? Be specific. What objects stand for other objects in the cartoons? Look through a number of cartoons and test your ability to recognize this technique. What symbols can you think of which you see daily at home or elsewhere?

14. Watch the editorial statements in your paper, in magazines, and on TV which all deal with the **the same problem,** such as the production of synthetic fuel in place of gasoline. Cut these statements out and post them on the bulletin board with the problem as the title heading. How many points of view can you find from different sources? You may even want to write out a quote from parents or friends.

15. Call this activity "News for Two." Choose a partner. Write five or more straight news sentences about anything which you select. Now rewrite those five sentences introducing opinion to see how they can be changed. Take turns reading each sentence to the class. First, one of you will read the **straight news** statement, then the other will read the **opinion statement.**

For example:

FACT   200 teen-agers attended the pop concert at Massey Hall.

OPINION 200 crazed teen-agers jammed into the otherwise respectable Massey Hall for a wild pop concert.

What key words changed the sentence from fact to opinion?

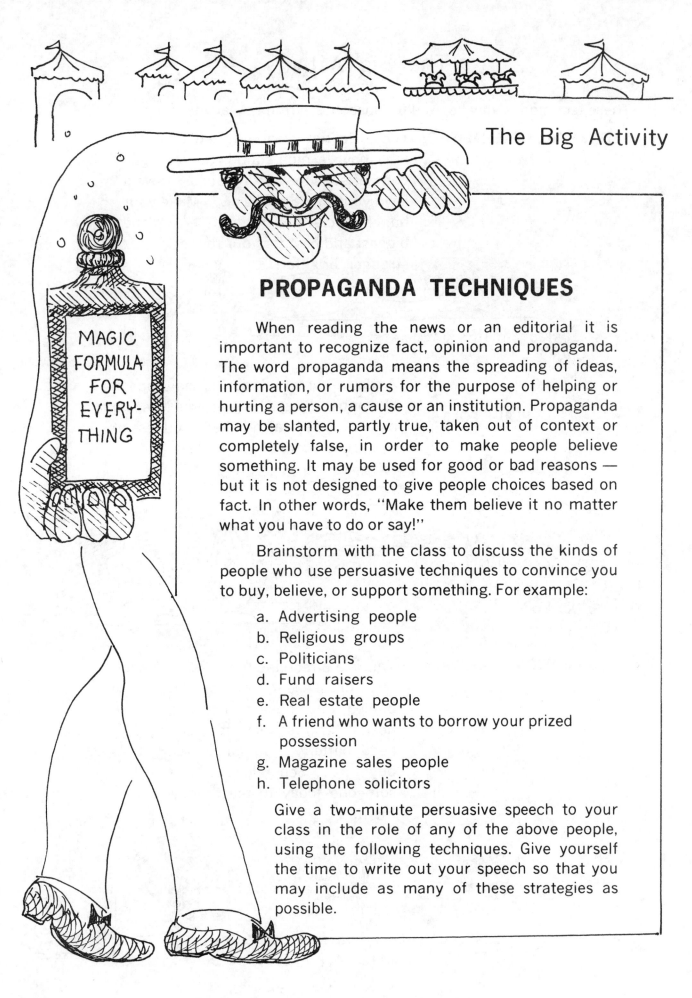

PROPAGANDA TECHNIQUES

When reading the news or an editorial it is important to recognize fact, opinion and propaganda. The word propaganda means the spreading of ideas, information, or rumors for the purpose of helping or hurting a person, a cause or an institution. Propaganda may be slanted, partly true, taken out of context or completely false, in order to make people believe something. It may be used for good or bad reasons — but it is not designed to give people choices based on fact. In other words, "Make them believe it no matter what you have to do or say!"

Brainstorm with the class to discuss the kinds of people who use persuasive techniques to convince you to buy, believe, or support something. For example:

a. Advertising people
b. Religious groups
c. Politicians
d. Fund raisers
e. Real estate people
f. A friend who wants to borrow your prized possession
g. Magazine sales people
h. Telephone solicitors

Give a two-minute persuasive speech to your class in the role of any of the above people, using the following techniques. Give yourself the time to write out your speech so that you may include as many of these strategies as possible.

MAGIC FORMULA FOR EVERYTHING

The Big Activity

These techniques may be used for speeches, writing, or advertising:

GLITTERING GENERALITIES: These do not mean a great deal but they have a nice sound. Some vague comparisons may be included. "Have a lawn you can be proud of." "Make your hair bouncier and fragrant." "Get the biggest and best for your money." ". . . stronger, brighter."

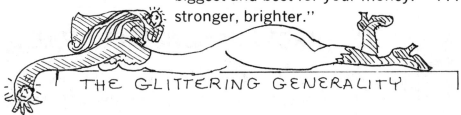

PLAIN FOLKS: A down-home, old-fashioned appeal. "Lemonade just like grandma used to make." "The hearth-baked goodness of whole grain bread."

EMOTIONAL APPEAL: This is a direct line to your fear, anger, pity, or sense of humor. "Don't be bullied into buying more than you need." "If you know the feeling of a dead battery on a lonely road, then buy . . ." "Send flowers to a certain someone today to tell them you love them."

The Big Activity

TESTIMONIAL: This refers to people who are either un-named, unknown, or famous who have something positive to say about a product. Everyone who is mentioned is made to sound like an expert! "Most experienced mothers depend upon . . ." "Jimmy Carson uses Apex tires," "Josephine Namath wears Gedilla stretch socks."

SCIENTIFIC APPROACH: Tests, statistics, surveys and pseudo-scientific jargon are used to be convincing. "Four out of five dentists use . . ." "A woman doctor researched the results of . . ." "Digestive upset can be blocked by the soothing effects of . . ." "Research shows . . ."

SNOB APPEAL: This gives the impression that people of elegance, wealth, good taste and intelligence will buy the seller's product. "When only the very best will do, buy . . ." "People of status understand that . . ." "If gracious living is important to you . . ."

The Big Activity

BANDWAGON: Since many people want to do what everybody else is doing, you are urged to hop aboard and join the crowd. "Be like all the others in your neighborhood and roller skate under the stars . . ." "Join the younger generation and drink dyspeptic cola."

TRANSFER: Grouping unrelated things for a stronger effect. The following combinations of traits do not necessarily go together! For example, young and joyous, thick and juicy, old and wise, homegrown and delicious, fat and funny, sophisticated and glamorous.

NAME-CALLING: Blaming problems on a particular group, person or idea. "The young punks stormed the principal's office like a pack of animals." "You know what adolescents are like." "The bad tempered senior citizens are complaining again." "I don't want those bigmouthed kids in the library."

CARD STACKING: To present only one side and hide the other. Only reveal what is favorable or only reveal what is unfavorable — whatever serves your cause. "It is not likely that these handsome, courteous boys from the best families in the community could be guilty of any wrongdoing!"

V. SPORTS

CONCEPT

SPORTS

Some Sports sections are like a paper within a paper. The Sports section may have its own editor, photographer, columnists and writers who have their own special field of expertise. Like page one, the Sports section features one important story.

The breadth of coverage appeals to a wide age and interest range because the newspaper covers professional, amateur, and school athletics, as well as individual sports stories.

Detailed averages, scores, standings and competitive results are an important part of the Sports section. These statistics are printed in smaller print called "agate" in order to get all the information in. "Agate nuts" are those readers who are addicted to reading this kind of information and may even go through standings with a magnifying glass. Listings of sports events which are in the regular section of the paper may also be included in this section. Reports on world sports and special events may be found as well.

Sports writers have special skills. They write rapidly and vividly. These people have strong feelings about the sports they cover and the fans who share their enthusiasm. Sports stories are fascinating because the games are preceded by much attention, controversy, and high-spirited speculation about the outcome. Men, women, and children share this passion for athletic games.

Sports writers are often faced with nerve-wracking deadlines for the morning paper. A game or a competition may end late at night with a news deadline for the writer from 10:45 p.m. to 11:15 p.m. The writer may have only two minutes after a game ends to report his story. All the background information may be written with two headlines — win or lose. In this way, the story is always ready to go.

Sportswriters use powerful descriptive language to capture the excitement of the game. They are known for their colorful verbs and adjectives in describing the action. They don't use ordinary words because it is much more thrilling to read that a team was **pulverized;** that someone **smashed** a homer; or that a **powerhouse** team **clobbered** the visitors.

Sports are packed with action, and so the Sports section is one of the most popularly read sections of the newspaper.

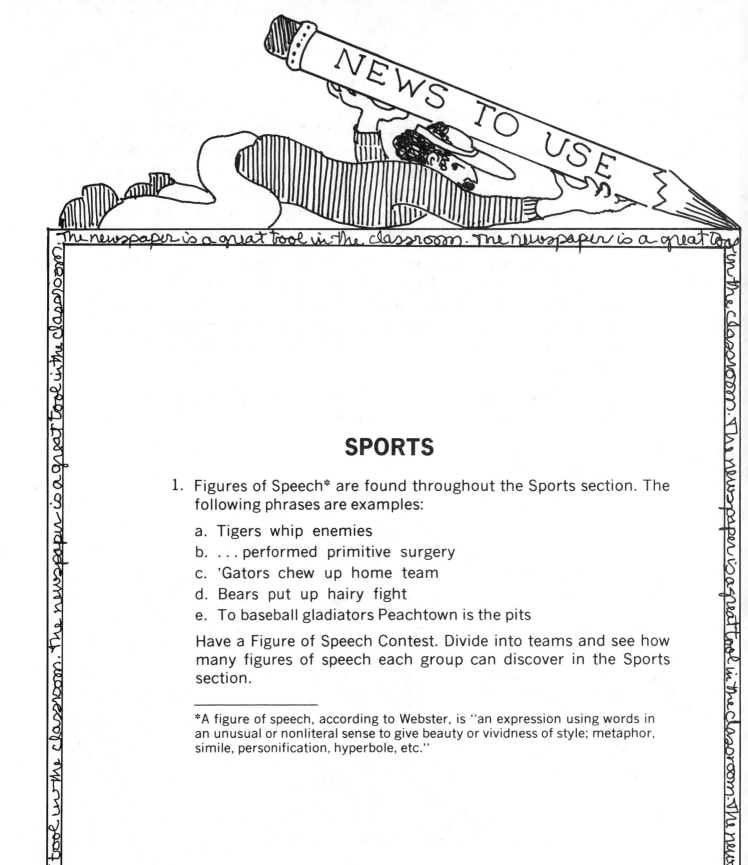

SPORTS

1. Figures of Speech* are found throughout the Sports section. The following phrases are examples:

   a. Tigers whip enemies
   b. ... performed primitive surgery
   c. 'Gators chew up home team
   d. Bears put up hairy fight
   e. To baseball gladiators Peachtown is the pits

   Have a Figure of Speech Contest. Divide into teams and see how many figures of speech each group can discover in the Sports section.

   _____

   *A figure of speech, according to Webster, is "an expression using words in an unusual or nonliteral sense to give beauty or vividness of style; metaphor, simile, personification, hyperbole, etc."

News to Use

2. Underline the colorful verbs found in the sports pages, such as crush, smash, whipped, bolster, roared, slump, fought, etc. Copy the sentences which include these verbs. Rewrite the sentences substituting the figure of speech with the literal or regular meaning. See how ordinary the sentence is without them. For example: "They won the game."

3. Make your own **Sports Word Search** for someone else to work on. Think of unusual games and sports words like jai alai (hi-li).

News to Use

DIRECTIONS: The words must always be in a straight line. Never skip a letter. The words may run forward, backward, up, down, diagonally.

```
A R C H E R Y L L A B T O O F
T M A R K C R I C K E T P Q S
R Q G S T E V E U A Z Q G I A
A N N R A U T O R A C I N G Y
C K I U T F L Z L O A N G G B
K Z L G O L F X I Y E K C O H
J G T B A D M I N T O N C J D
O N S Y A S X G G N I H S I F
G I E H T S O G N I T A K S I
G F R L Q N E C Z I J D H R S
I R W U J N B B C X L E U P K
N U A T E R G G A E E W M I I
G S A I L I N G W L R N O Q I
H V V O L L E Y B A L L L B N
S W I M M I N G H U N T I N G
```

CLUES:

HOCKEY	BADMINTON	SOCCER	BASEBALL	FISHING
TENNIS	VOLLEYBALL	TRACK	CURLING	SWIMMING
SAILING	SQUASH	CRICKET	GOLF	FOOTBALL
BOWLING	SKATING	SKIING	HUNTING	AUTO RACING
WRESTLING	JOGGING	ARCHERY	SURFING	RUGBY

4. Follow the scores of your favorite team. List the daily game results. Give the average score for the week.

5. Plot on graph paper the number of points earned daily by two teams in the same league for a week. What team scored the most points?

6. Find something in the Sports section and research an interesting fact(s) about it. For example: There are 336 dimples on a golf ball. The dimpled cover helps make the ball's flight accurate and far. The game was developed in the year 1100 in Scotland and was based on a Roman game. Every year more than 16 million people play golf in the USA.

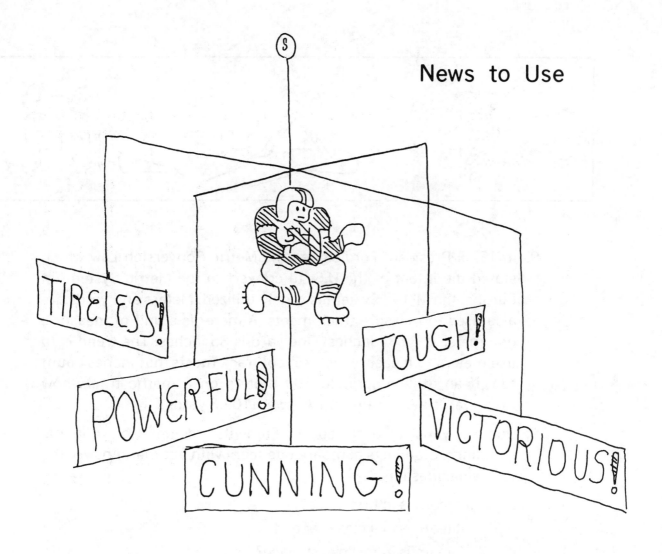

7. Make a sports adjective collage or mobile. Cut out the adjectives and paste them around a scene of the sports event.

8. Teen-agers' favorite games are basketball, swimming, bowling, baseball and roller skating. Create an acrostic description of your favorite game.

A TENNIS ACROSTIC

T EAMWORK
E NERGETIC
N ET
N IMBLE
I NSTRUCTOR
S ERVE

9. In 1975, President Ford signed the Metric Conversion Law which stated the intent of the U.S. to convert to the Metric System. In Europe, the Metric System is widely utilized. Meters and yards are also used to measure track meets. A meter is a unit of measure; one meter is 39.37 inches. One yard is 36 inches. The trend is to use meters to measure high school track meets, but inches count too. If an athlete sprinted 100 meters on a metric track, how many yards did he/she run? Answer (109.3 yards)

10. Choose your favorite sport. Find its regional or national standings. Standings compare one team with another. Answer the following questions:

a) What team is in first place?

b) What team is in a close second?

c) What team is in the lowest place?

d) Compute the average score of the winning team.

e) Create your own math problem from the sports standings listed in your newspaper. First work out the problem with the correct answer. Then choose a friend and ask him to solve your problem.

11. Here are some official starting signals for various athletic events. Identify the sport each belongs to. Add some of your own to the list.

"Gentlemen, start your engines."

"Play ball!"

"On your mark, get set, go!"

"And they're off!"

"Shake hands and come out fighting."

Are there other terms and sayings that belong to a particular sport? Look through your paper and identify them.

12. Abbreviations are found throughout the Sports section, such as FG (field goal in soccer) or FT (free throw in basketball). Find as many of these abbreviations as you can and identify them according to the sports and their meanings.

13. Make up your own new game and give it a name. Describe the game, number of players, scoring, and rules in written form. Test the game by first explaining it to your classmates and then actually playing it. After the game is played, what would you change to improve the rules or the point of the game?

14. "It isn't whether you win or lose, it's how you play the game!" Many people have heard that old saying. What do you think it means? Do you agree? How do you feel about competition in school? How can we have competiton **and** cooperation at the same time? What kinds of competition do we read and hear about outside of school?

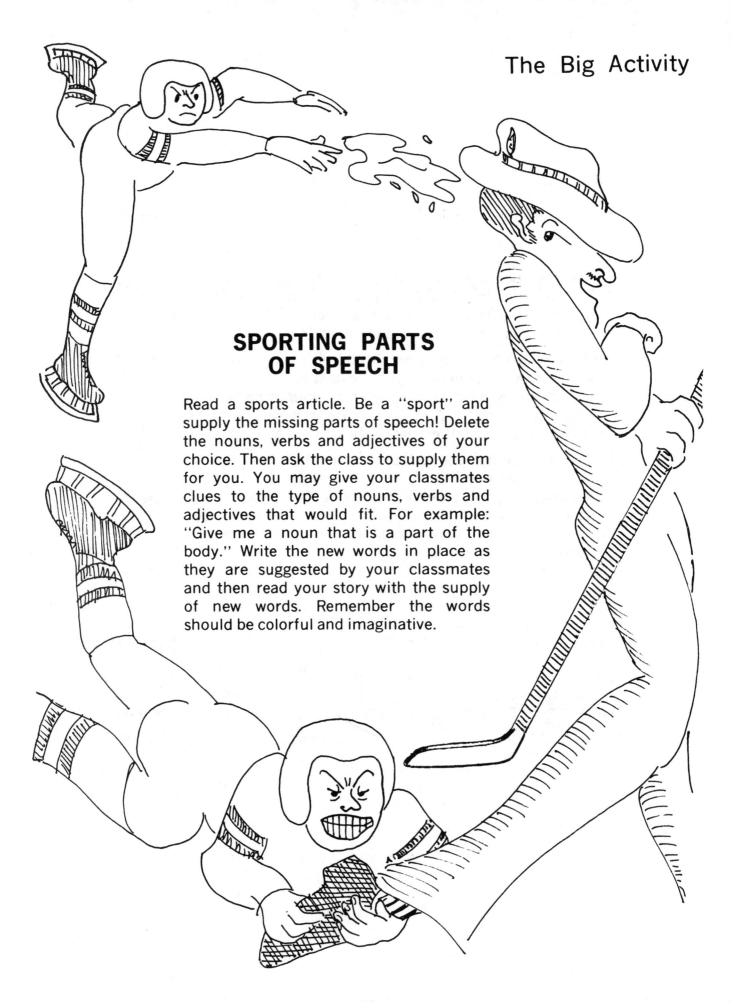

SPORTING PARTS OF SPEECH

Read a sports article. Be a "sport" and supply the missing parts of speech! Delete the nouns, verbs and adjectives of your choice. Then ask the class to supply them for you. You may give your classmates clues to the type of nouns, verbs and adjectives that would fit. For example: "Give me a noun that is a part of the body." Write the new words in place as they are suggested by your classmates and then read your story with the supply of new words. Remember the words should be colorful and imaginative.

For example:

Hockey is a (**violent**) game. A lot of fans think it should be
          adjective

controlled by the (**leagues**). There are (**crushing**) body checks, and
          plural noun   adjective

free-for-all (**fights**). Last week (**Sandy**) McNertney, a member of the
          plural noun   proper noun

(**Podunk**) Pistols, punched a patron in the (**nose**) because the patron
proper n.   noun—part of the body

stole his hockey stick. McNertney chased the thief with a (**wet**) (**towel**),
                    adj.   noun

right up to the (**refreshment**) stand and (**knocked**) him to the floor.
          noun—type of food   verb (past tense)

Another player removed the patron's (**shoe**) and bounced it off his
                noun

(**head**). Then the (**angry**) player (**ran**) and grabbed him by his (**skinny**)
n.—part of body   adj.   verb (p. tense)   adjective

throat. This is not a (**funny**) story. Let's take the violence out of
          adjective

hockey. It will make us (**better**) fans and (**better**) players. It's no joke!
          adjective   adjective

VI. COMICS

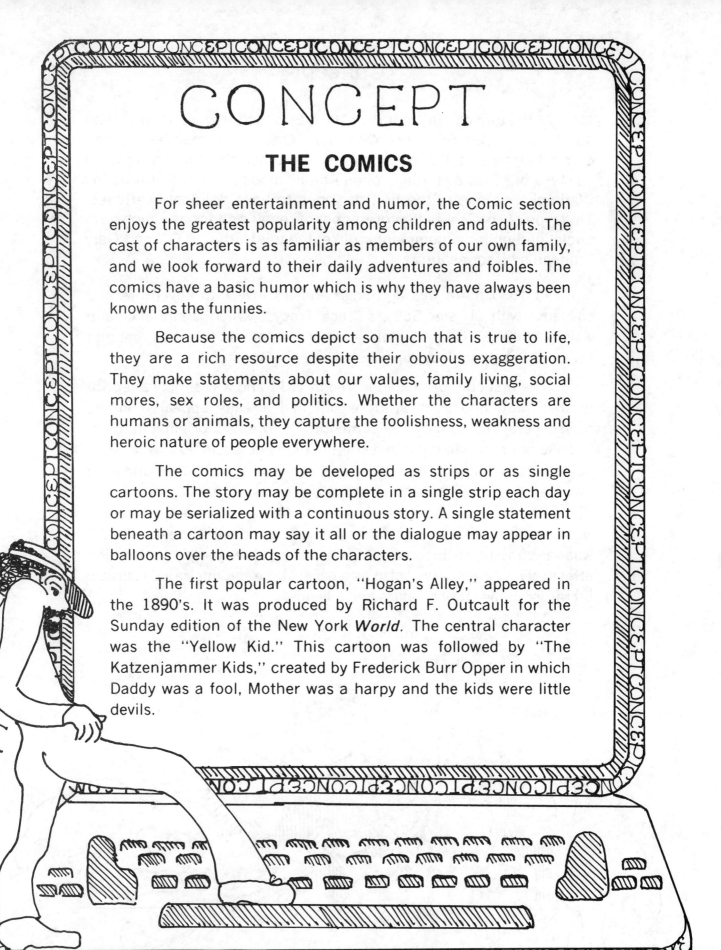

CONCEPT

THE COMICS

For sheer entertainment and humor, the Comic section enjoys the greatest popularity among children and adults. The cast of characters is as familiar as members of our own family, and we look forward to their daily adventures and foibles. The comics have a basic humor which is why they have always been known as the funnies.

Because the comics depict so much that is true to life, they are a rich resource despite their obvious exaggeration. They make statements about our values, family living, social mores, sex roles, and politics. Whether the characters are humans or animals, they capture the foolishness, weakness and heroic nature of people everywhere.

The comics may be developed as strips or as single cartoons. The story may be complete in a single strip each day or may be serialized with a continuous story. A single statement beneath a cartoon may say it all or the dialogue may appear in balloons over the heads of the characters.

The first popular cartoon, "Hogan's Alley," appeared in the 1890's. It was produced by Richard F. Outcault for the Sunday edition of the New York *World.* The central character was the "Yellow Kid." This cartoon was followed by "The Katzenjammer Kids," created by Frederick Burr Opper in which Daddy was a fool, Mother was a harpy and the kids were little devils.

Concept

At the turn of the century in 1907, Bud Fisher created "Mutt and Jeff" for the *San Francisco Chronicle*. One of the members of the comic team was tall and skinny and the other short and stubby. In 1924 Harold Gray's "Little Orphan Annie" made its debut with Daddy Warbucks, as one of the first cartoons to have political overtones. This type of comic was the forerunner of today's cartoons which have social and political commentary like Johnny Hart's "B.C." and Gary Trudeau's "Doonesbury."

In 1930 there was a change and a move into adventure and suspense with Chester Gould's "Dick Tracy," which is still alive and well in America's comic pages — along with others like the great and revered "Superman" by Jerry Siegel and Joe Shuster.

The first comic book appeared in 1911 and was simply a reprint of the "Mutt and Jeff" strips which had already appeared in the newspapers. The comic book came into its own with original material in 1935 but began to fall into disrepute in the 40's and 50's because of objectionable subject matter. By this time the field had expanded to include all types of adventure stories, dramas, romance and horror. World War II served as a great impetus to the comic book field since it was also used as a format for training and industrial instruction. It was a superficial medium, but captured the reader's attention effectively. Comics served also as a new source for illustrated classical literature, Bible stories, fables and legends.

Concept

In 1954, responding to public protest, comic book publishers adopted the Comics Code Authority which monitored objectionable content. In the 1960's there was a resurgence of interest in comics which had appeal for children as well as sophisticated adults. An example of this kind of appealing strip is Charles Schultz's "Peanuts" with our engaging friends, Charlie Brown, Snoopy, Lucy, Linus and Schroeder.

Interestingly, there are a few papers like the *New York Times,* the *Wall Street Journal* and *The Christian Science Monitor* which do not have comics. Still the popularity of this form is so great that comic figures, because of their familiarity, are used widely in advertising. Comics are also the source for movies, plays, TV programs and pop art. "Annie," "Superman," "Wonder Woman" and "Tarzan," to name a few, have been immortalized in America.

Our language, too, has been imprinted by expressions from the comic strips.

Comics are clearly a big business and require considerable work and production time. The story and illustrations can be the work of one person or sometimes it is a team effort. The comic strip is completed about six weeks before publication and then is sent to a syndicate for sales and distribution. A syndicate is a company which contracts to act as the agent for the cartoonist. The syndicate takes care of financial arrangements and distribution to newspapers worldwide. A look at any comic strip will show a date, which designates when the strip is to appear. The name of the syndicate and the author(s) also appears.

An acknowledgement of the comics as a mirror held up to life offers humor, realism and satire for classroom activities and discussion.

COMICS

1. A syndicate may mail several installments of a comic strip to a newspaper at one time. The newspaper is required to print these strips according to the release date printed on the strip. Find the dates and the cartoonist's name on five comic strips and write them down. Look carefully.

2. On the comic strips find the names of as many syndicates as possible which act as agents or distributors for the cartoonists. List them with the class on the board. How many syndicates have been found?

3. Find a comic which deals with a family problem. Cut it out and describe the nature of the problem to the class. Is it funny or serious? How do you feel about that particular problem?

4. How many different topics can you identify in the comics? Which ones would you classify as:

   a. Family living
   b. Animals that act like humans
   c. Historical
   d. Political
   e. Science fiction
   f. Spooky
   g. Adventure
   h. Career

5. How many different careers can you identify in the comics? In what careers are the characters men? The women? What roles do the men or boys fill that the women or girls could not fill? Discuss.

6. Choose a partner. Pick out a comic strip for the day which has funny dialogue. Assign a character to each other. Read the dialogue as it appears. You have now prepared a skit for two, with each of you taking a part. Rehearse and present it to the class along with other "Comic Duets."

7. Look through the comic strips to find contractions. Write all that you can find on a piece of paper. Next to each contraction write the two words the contraction stands for.

8. Arrange an introduction between your favorite characters from different comic strips. "What if Snoopy Met Superman?" Write a paragraph which describes their reactions, conversations or adventures in a brief meeting.

9. Rewrite the dialogue in the comic balloons for one strip. Indicate the speaker and add the quotation marks. Remember to include: he said, she replied, they shouted, etc. Substitute the slang words with standard English if there is an opportunity. For example:

CORKY: "I'm hatin' to say it but I got no money to pay ya."

Correction: "I hate to say it," said Corky, "but I have no money to pay you!"

SAM: " 'Member you always sayin' you pay your bills good? Ain't that what you said, huh?"

Correction: "Remember," replied Sam, "you always said you paid your bills on time. Isn't that what you always said?"

News to Use

10. Find an action or adventure comic for one day. Cut it out and paste it on a piece of paper. Title it "The Further Adventures of (**your choice**)." Develop the story creatively. What will happen next?

11. Select a comic strip. Cut it out and separate the pictures. Cut out the conversation balloons, too. Exchange the pictures with a partner. Arrange the sequence of pictures and fill in the conversation. A simpler class activity can be developed by eliminating the dialogue balloons and showing the strips on a screen with an opaque projector. The whole class can speculate on the conversation!

12. Read "Peanuts" for about a week. Cut out a panel daily and save it. Reread it. Though it seems like just a fun comic, what is there about it that resembles real life? Think about friendship, honesty, joy, success and personal problems such as shyness, loneliness and fear.

13. Onomatopoeia is a term for words which describe sounds. The comics are full of them! How many can you find? For example: Zap! Slurp! Squish! Bong! Slam! Tsk, Tsk! See how long a list you can make by adding your own. Who will be the Onomatopoeia Champion of the class?

The Big Activity

INGMAR THE INCREDIBLE

CARTOON CONSONANTS

The following are titles of popular comic strips which are all mixed up. In order to identify them you must fill in the missing consonants. The vowels which appear are the only clues. Look out! How many can you work out? How many of these syndicated strips can be found in your daily or Sunday paper?

1. DOONESBURY   (_ o _ _ e _ _ o _ a _)
2. DICK TRACY   (_ _ o _ _ i e)
3. SUPERMAN   (_ e e _ _ e _ a i _ e _)
4. POGO   (_ o _ _ i)
5. BEETLE BAILEY   (_ i _ _ _ _ a _ _)
6. MARMADUKE   (_ e a _ u _ _)
7. PEANUTS   (_ a _ _ a _ u _ e)
8. HAGAR THE HORRIBLE (_ i _ a _ _ o _ i _)
9. NANCY   (_ _ e _ _ a _ _ a _ _)
10. BRENDA STARR   (_ a _ _)
11. GASOLINE ALLEY   (_ a _ a _ _ _ e _ o _ _ i _ _ e)
12. BLONDIE   (_ u _ e _ _ a _)
13. DONDI   (_ a _ o _ i _ e a _ _ e _)
14. WIZARD OF ID   (_ o o _ e _ _ u _ _)
15. WONDER WOMAN   (_ o _ o)

the weather

Detroit area forecast: Clear to partly cloudy Monday, with a high near 40. Lows Monday night in the 20s. Northerly winds at 5 to 15 m.p.h. will be light and variable.

For local weather at anytime, call 932-1212 or 932-8437.

RECENT DETROIT TEMPERATURES

Date	3/16	3/17	3/18	3/19	3/20	3/21
High	34	35	32	28	39	44
Low	20	22	15	21	23	25

TRAVELERS' FORECASTS

Chicago: Chance of showers Tuesday. Partly cloudy Wednesday. Lows in the lower 30s to lower 40s. Highs in the upper 40s to mid-50s. Fair and warmer Thursday. Lows in the 30s. Highs in the lower 50s to lower 60s.

Miami: Chance of showers Tuesday and Wednesday. Fair and cooler Thursday. Lows averaging in the 60s. Highs near 80.

Denver: Little or no precipitation expected Tuesday through Thursday with a warming trend. Highs from 55 to 65 and in the 40s in the mountains. Lows from 25 to 35 and from 10 to 20 in the mountains.

Phoenix: Fair Tuesday and Wednesday. Cloudy Thursday Highs in the 50s in the mountains and in the mid-80s in the deserts. Lows in the 20s in the mountains and the mid-40s to mid-50s in the deserts.

Los Angeles: Fair Tuesday. Cooler Wednesday and Thursday. Highs in coastal areas from 65 to 73, then cooling about five degrees. Lows from 42 to 54. Mountain highs from 45 to 55. Lows from 20 to 35.

TODAY'S U.S. CITY FORECASTS

CITY	WEA	HI/LO	CITY	WEA	HI/LO
Albany	ptcldy	43/29	Kansas City	sunny	55/36
Albuquerque	fair	68/32	Las Vegas	fair	73/45
Amarillo	fair	64/35	Little Rock	sunny	61/39
Anchorage	cloudy	35/25	Los Angeles	fair	72/52
Asheville	cloudy	46/35	Louisville	ptcldy	55/36
Atlanta	ptcldy	59/34	Memphis	ptcldy	59/39
Atlantic C	cloudy	42/31	Miami Beach	sunny	79/54
Austin	fair	71/44	Milwaukee	sunny	44/30
Baltimore	cloudy	46/34	Mpls/S.Paul	sunny	51/30
Billings	ptcldy	50/30	Nashville	ptcldy	57/33
Birmingham	ptcldy	62/31	New Orleans	ptcldy	65/45
Bismarck	ptcldy	51/28	New York	ptcldy	48/36
Boise	fair	60/38	Norfolk	rain	45/38
Boston	sunny	43/37	Ok'ma City	sunny	62/38
Buffalo	ptcldy	43/26	Omaha	sunny	54/34
Casper	ptcldy	48/26	Orlando	sunny	73/45
Char'ton SC	rain	55/38	Phi'delphia	cloudy	46/32
Char'ton WV	sunny	53/28	Phoenix	sunny	83/53
Charlotte	cloudy	50/38	Pittsburgh	ptcldy	48/27
Cheyenne	ptcldy	49/26	Portland Me	sunny	44/25
Chicago	sunny	49/32	Portland Or	ptcldy	62/44
Cincinnati	sunny	54/29	Providence	sunny	45/31
Cleveland	sunny	45/27	Raleigh	shwrs	49/37
Columbia SC	cloudy	54/30	Rapid City	ptcldy	65/35
Columbus Oh	sunny	50/29	Reno	fair	62/29
Dal/Ft'Worth	fair	66/40	Richmond	cloudy	45/37
Dayton	sunny	52/30	St Louis	sunny	54/34
Denver	ptcldy	55/30	St Pt/Tampa	sunny	70/49
Des Moines	sunny	55/30	Salt Lake C	ptcldy	57/36
Duluth	sunny	40/20	San Antonio	fair	73/42
El Paso	fair	75/38	San Diego	fair	72/55
Fairbanks	cloudy	25/19	San Fr'sco	ptcldy	66/50
Fargo	ptcldy	46/26	San Juan PR	ptcldy	86/76
Flagstaff	sunny	57/24	Seattle	ptcldy	59/45
Hartford	sunny	47/30	Shreveport	ptcldy	68/41
Helena	sunny	52/28	Spokane	ptcldy	57/37
Honolulu	sunny	81/65	Syracuse	ptcldy	44/26
Houston	fair	71/42	Tucson	sunny	79/49
Ind'apolis	sunny	52/29	Tulsa	sunny	61/40
Jacks'ville	ptcldy	62/41	Washington	cloudy	48/37
Juneau	cloudy	42/37	Wichita	ptcldy	61/37

TODAY'S CANADIAN FORECASTS

CITY	WEA	HI/LO	CITY	WEA	HI/LO
Edmonton	NA	NA	Regina	ptcldy	36/18
Victoria	cloudy	54/41	St. Johns	cloudy	26/23
Halifax	sunny	37/25	Toronto	ptcldy	41/26
Quebec City	ptcldy	39/25	Vancouver	cloudy	54/43
Montreal	cloudy	41/30	Winnipeg	sunny	32/21

EXTENDED OUTLOOK

For the Detroit area: Little or no precipitation is expected Tuesday through Thursday. There will be minor day-to-day temperature changes. Highs will range mainly in the 40s, lows in the mid-20s to low 30s.

CLIMATIC ALMANAC

Temperatures: Sunday's high 45, low 23. Records for the date: high 81 (1938), low 3 (1885). One year ago Monday: high 40, low 33. Departure from normal since Jan. 1: minus 123.

Precipitation: Sunday: none. Total for March: .12 in. Total for this year: 3.82 ins.

Snowfall: Sunday: none. Total for March: .6 in. Total this season: 38.4 ins.

Heating degree days: Sunday: 31. Normal: 33. Season: 5,856. (Degree days equal the difference between the mean temperature for the day and 65 degrees.)

Wayne County pollution index at 2 p.m. Friday: downtown Detroit, 53, light contamination (dust). Highest outside downtown was in southwest Detroit, 61, light contamination (dust).

Sun rises Monday at 6:32 a.m., sets at 6:49 p.m.

Phases of the moon: Last quarter, March 28; new moon, April 4; first quarter, April 11; full moon, April 19. Moon rises Monday at 9:47 p.m., sets at 8:14 a.m.

AROUND THE WORLD YESTERDAY

CITY	HI/LO	CITY	HI/LO	CITY	HI/LO
Amsterdam	50/41	Geneva	64/37	Oslo	34/32
Athens	70/48	Hong Kong	68/66	Paris	61/52
Beirut	68/60	Jerusalem	56/45	Rio	82/68
Belgrade	66/45	Jo'burg	72/56	Rome	63/39
Berlin	66/45	Lisbon	63/52	Sao Paulo	75/63
Bogota	70/45	London	55/49	Singapore	88/75
Brussels	55/39	Madrid	63/43	Stockholm	33/19
Cairo	75/52	Manila	95/75	Sydney	73/66
Copenhagen	48/46	Moscow	43/34	Tel Aviv	68/54
Dublin	50/41	New Delhi	81/59	Tokyo	59/48
Frankfurt	66/36	Nicosia	66/48	Vienna	64/43

MICHIGAN FORECAST

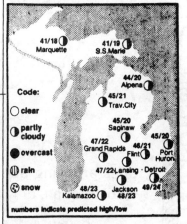

Sunday's Michigan high was 50 at Kalamazoo and Jackson; the low was 14 at Marquette.

Lower Peninsula: Clear to partly cloudy Monday, high near 40. Low Monday night around 20. Little or no precipitation expected Tuesday through Thursday. Minor day-to-day temperature changes. Highs mainly in the 40s, lows in the mid-20s to low 30s.

Upper Peninsula: Clear to partly cloudy Monday, high near 40. Lows Monday night around 20. Little or no precipitation expected Tuesday through Thursday. Minor day-to-day temperature changes. Highs ranging in the 40s, lows in the mid-20s to lower 30s.

SKI CONDITIONS (base in inches)

West: Boyne Country up to 29. Crystal Mt. 10-38. Nub's Nob up to 21. Sugar Loaf 12-36.

Closed for the season: Alpine Valley, Black Forest, Mt. Brighton, Mt. Grampian, Mt. Holly, Pine Knob, Riverview Highlands, Caberfae, Bintz Apple Mountain, Sylvan Knob, Skyline, Cannonsburg, Tyrolean Hills, Traverse City Holiday, Mt. Maria, Royal Valley, Schuss Mountain, Shanty Creek, Swiss Valley, Mt. Mancelona, Timber Ridge and Timberlee.

Skiers are advised to telephone ahead for reports on slope conditions.

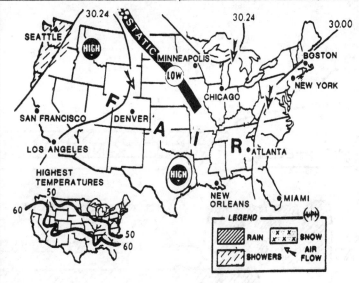

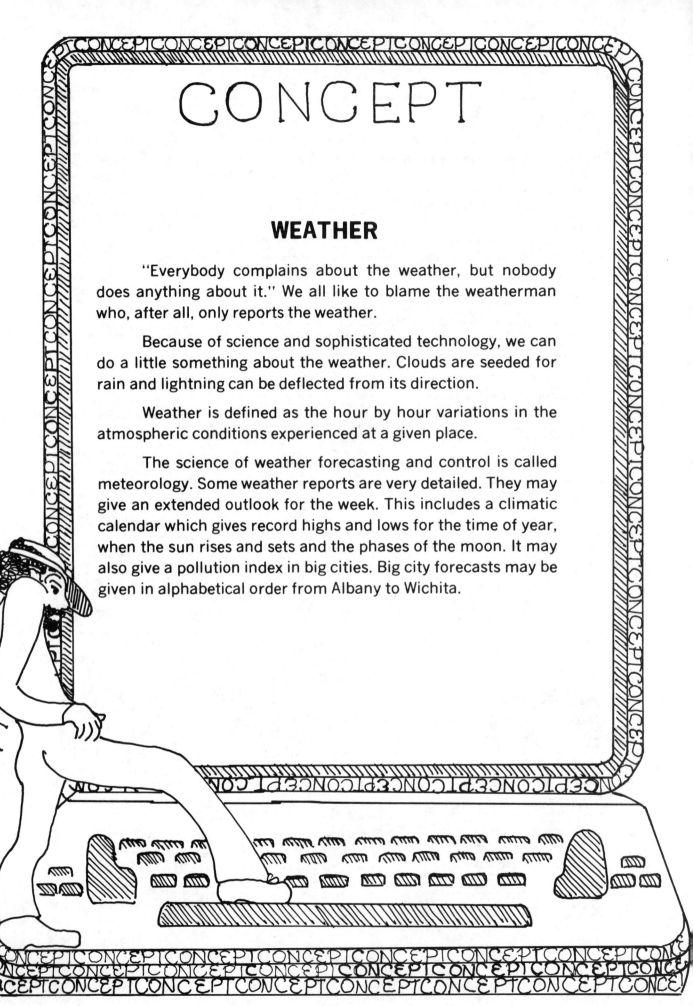

CONCEPT

WEATHER

"Everybody complains about the weather, but nobody does anything about it." We all like to blame the weatherman who, after all, only reports the weather.

Because of science and sophisticated technology, we can do a little something about the weather. Clouds are seeded for rain and lightning can be deflected from its direction.

Weather is defined as the hour by hour variations in the atmospheric conditions experienced at a given place.

The science of weather forecasting and control is called meteorology. Some weather reports are very detailed. They may give an extended outlook for the week. This includes a climatic calendar which gives record highs and lows for the time of year, when the sun rises and sets and the phases of the moon. It may also give a pollution index in big cities. Big city forecasts may be given in alphabetical order from Albany to Wichita.

Concept

The National Weather Service is part of the Environmental Science Services Administration (ESSA) of the U.S. Department of Commerce. It is located near the National Meteorological Center in Washington, D.C. Here, data from over 300 U.S. weather stations are charted and distributed to forecast centers throughout the country.

Balloons, conventional aircraft and satellites are sources used to determine long and short-range forecasts. These sources provide information about hurricanes, tornadoes and other dangerous weather conditions.

If you live near the ocean, the report will include information about high and low tides and surf conditions. If you live near the Great Lakes, information will include lake conditions for recreational and commercial boats. Precipitation (rain or snow) will be predicted with totals for each month.

A national weather map may be included in your newspaper with a pictorial legend of markings on the map.

If you have special plans for the day or weekend, you may want to check your newspaper for the daily or long-range forecast of the place you will be visiting.

We are all affected by the weather. Although science is used to study and track its movement and direction, we still find it mysterious and exciting.

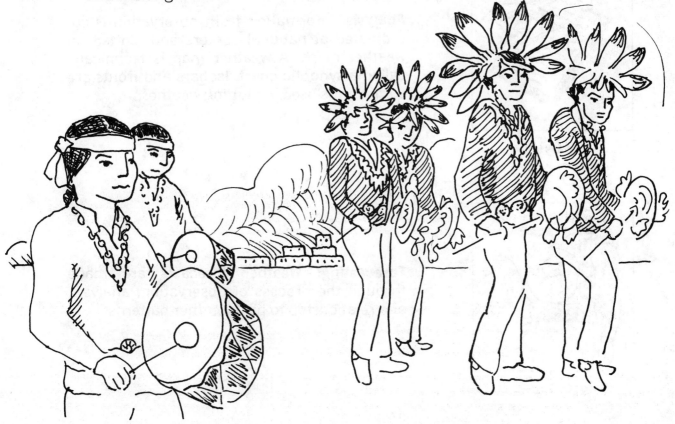

THREE STAGES OF WEATHER FORECASTING

Did you know there are three basic steps all forecasters use in predicting the weather?

These steps are:

1. Observation
2. Analysis
3. Forecasting

Observation

Observation: Includes 24-hour weather watching and the gathering of data of weather conditions over land and sea. Weather satellites and radio sounds are used in this process.

Analysis

Analysis: Information from observation is coordinated at national centers and plotted on weather maps. A weather map is technically called a synoptic chart. Isobars and fronts are some terms used in plotting weather.

Forecasting

Forecasting: Weather forecasts are made through the process of observation, analysis, and relationship to past weather patterns.

CONCEPT

HOW AIR TRAVELS

Air moves in strange and mysterious ways. Objects move through air because of the special characteristics of air: air movement (wind), air pressure, and air compression.

Air moves for many reasons. The rotation of the earth creates the CORIOLIS FORCE. In the northern hemisphere, this force pushes air currents to the right of the direction in which they are moving. In the southern hemisphere, the Coriolis Force pushes air currents to the left.

The gravitational force of the sun and moon also moves air. **Tides** of air occur just as regularly as water tides.

Air is filled with molecules. The vibration of these molecules in the gases of the air also causes the movement of air.

Another characteristic of air is that it resists the motion of objects going through it. The faster something moves through the air the more air resistance it meets. The faster you run, the greater air resistance against your body. One of the reasons a piece of paper will not fall straight down is because it keeps rubbing against the air. The paper will flutter between the molecules of the air.

All of these forces cause air to move and affect any objects that pass through it. (See The Big Activity, HELIUM BALLOON MESSAGES.)

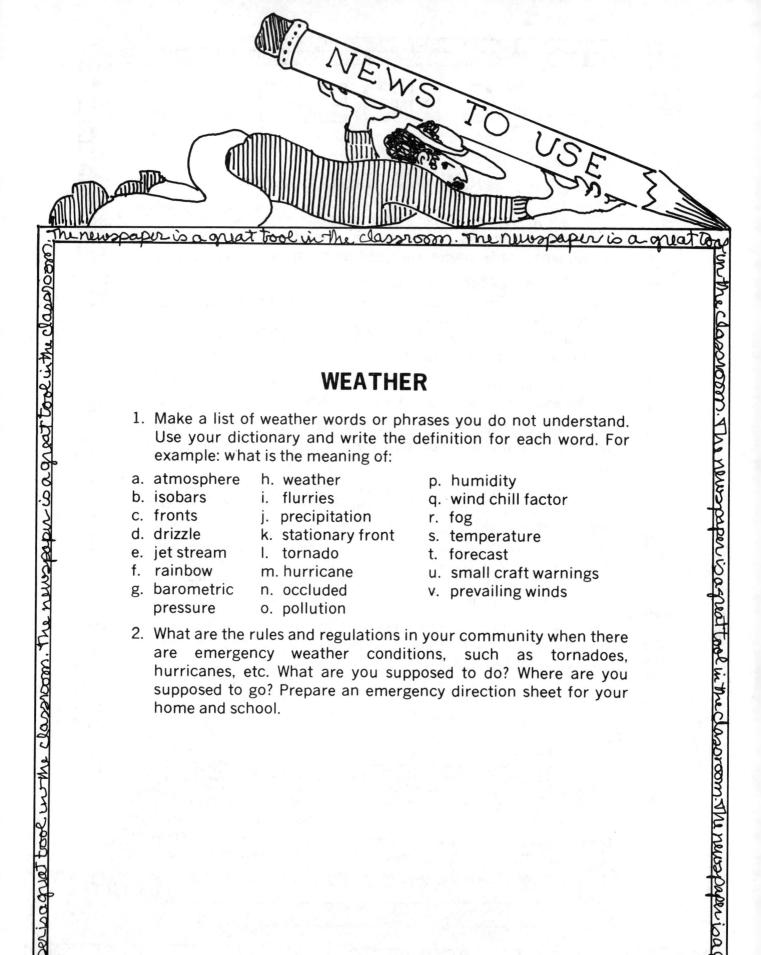

WEATHER

1. Make a list of weather words or phrases you do not understand. Use your dictionary and write the definition for each word. For example: what is the meaning of:

a. atmosphere
b. isobars
c. fronts
d. drizzle
e. jet stream
f. rainbow
g. barometric pressure

h. weather
i. flurries
j. precipitation
k. stationary front
l. tornado
m. hurricane
n. occluded
o. pollution

p. humidity
q. wind chill factor
r. fog
s. temperature
t. forecast
u. small craft warnings
v. prevailing winds

2. What are the rules and regulations in your community when there are emergency weather conditions, such as tornadoes, hurricanes, etc. What are you supposed to do? Where are you supposed to go? Prepare an emergency direction sheet for your home and school.

News to Use

3. How many inventions can you discover that were used in weather forecasting in ancient times? In modern times? (weather vanes, rain gauges, satellites, balloons, radar, etc.)

4. What are the rules about safety in an electrical storm? How does lightning strike out-of-doors? What safety rule should you know about "downed" power lines?

5. What does a barometer tell you? Write your answer in as few sentences as possible.

6. Can you think of any weather predictions from old sayings that are not scientific: "Red sky at night — sailors' delight"?

7. Look at the weather forecast in your newspaper. How many different kinds of information does it give? State five facts that interest you.

8. If you wanted to ski, what city would you want to be in according to today's weather? If you wanted to swim, what city would you want to be in?

9. Graph the temperatures of ten cities for one week. Identify the coldest and hottest city on your graph.

10. When does the sun rise and set today? When does the moon rise and set today? What phase is the moon in today?

News to Use

11. Have you ever felt colder than the thermometer indicates? This is not just your imagination. It could be the **wind chill factor,** the combination of the wind velocity and the temperature which together increase the feeling of cold.

To find out how cold it **really** is, the chart below will help you find the answer. This chart is an example of one used in a cold climate.

For example, if the actual thermometer reading is 20° and the wind velocity is 10 miles per hour (MPH) the equivalent temperature, considering the wind chill factor is 2°.

If the actual thermometer reading is 20° and the wind velocity is 30 miles per hour (MPH) then the equivalent temperature, considering the wind chill factor is -18°.

WIND CHILL FACTOR

ACTUAL THERMOMETER READING

	35	30	25	20	15	10	5	0	-5	-10
EQUIVALENT TEMPERATURE										
0	35	30	25	20	15	10	5	0	-5	-10
10	21	16	9	2	-2	-9	-15	-22	-27	-31
20	12	3	-4	-9	-17	-24	-32	-40	-46	-52
30	5	-2	-11	-18	-26	-33	-41	-49	-56	-63
40	1	-4	-15	-22	-29	-36	-45	-54	-62	-69
50	0	-7	-17	-24	-31	-38	-47	-56	-63	-70

Wind Velocity in MPH

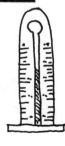

12. Historically the U.S. has always used the Fahrenheit scale. Because the world is moving toward uniformity in measurement, the U.S. is now adopting the use of the Celsius scale as part of its conversion to the metric system.

Celsius to Fahrenheit

Here is an easy conversion chart which changes Celsius (formerly centigrade) to Fahrenheit. The Fahrenheit figures are rounded off.

CEL.	FAHR.
5	41
6	43
7	45
8	46½
9	48
10	50
11	52
12	53½
13	55½
14	57
15	59
16	61
17	62½
18	64½
19	66
20	68
21	70
22	71½
23	73
24	75
25	77
26	79
27	80½
28	82
29	84
30	86
31	88
32	90
33	92
34	93½
35	95
36	97
37	98½
38	100

The formula for converting C to F: (Celsius temperature x 1.8) + 32 = F

The formula for converting Fahrenheit to Celsius: Fahrenheit temperature: (F - 32°) x .55 = C

The **Celsius System** is named after Anders Celsius (1701-1744), a Swedish astronomer who proposed the centigrade (Celsius) temperature scale which has 0°C for the freezing point and 100°C for the boiling point of water.

The **Fahrenheit System** was named after Gabriel Daniel Fahrenheit (1686-1736), a Dutch instrument maker who invented the mercury-in-glass thermometer. In the Fahrenheit temperature the freezing point of water is 32°F and the boiling point is 212°F.

Now, make two conversions from Celsius to Fahrenheit using the formula. Make two conversions from Fahrenheit to Celsius using the formula. Check the chart for correct answers.

The Big Activity

HELIUM BALLOON MESSAGES

To demonstrate the wonders of air movement and the objects that float through it, send up your own helium* balloon! Find out how far the wind and air currents will carry it. Enclose your "Air Mail" message with the date, your name, school address and room number. Indicate that this is a weather experiment your class is conducting. Ask the finder to please write a note back to you indicating what city and state the balloon was found in. Ask for additional information or comments.

IMPORTANT! On the day of the flight, wait for a day with a vigorous breeze to give the balloon every flight advantage. Launch the balloons from the playground or a safe place **away from trees and traffic.** Once released, the balloons are free spirits. Do not run after them!

When the class has received some answers from the "finders," write a human interest story about your weather experiment for a local paper or your class paper including the results, whether they be startling or disappointing. (See The Concept, HOW AIR TRAVELS.)

---

* Helium can be purchased in tanks (as seen at state fairs, etc.). Look in the Yellow Pages of your telephone book under "Balloons."

The Big Activity

HELIUM BALLOON MESSAGE — FOR FUN AND SCIENCE

Type or write with waterproof ink. Enclose your message in a plastic bag. Tie it securely with string to the neck of your balloon.

DATE _____

MY NAME _____

SCHOOL _____ GRADE ____ ROOM ____

SCHOOL ADDRESS _____

CITY _____ STATE _____ ZIP _____

MESSAGE:

MANY THANKS FOR YOUR COOPERATION ON
BEHALF OF OUR CLASS!!

FINDER'S NAME _____

ADDRESS _____

CITY _____ STATE _____ ZIP _____

TIME FOUND _____ DATE _____

PLACE FOUND _____

RETURN MESSAGE:

When you find the balloon, please send your message back to the address above.

VIII. BUSINESS

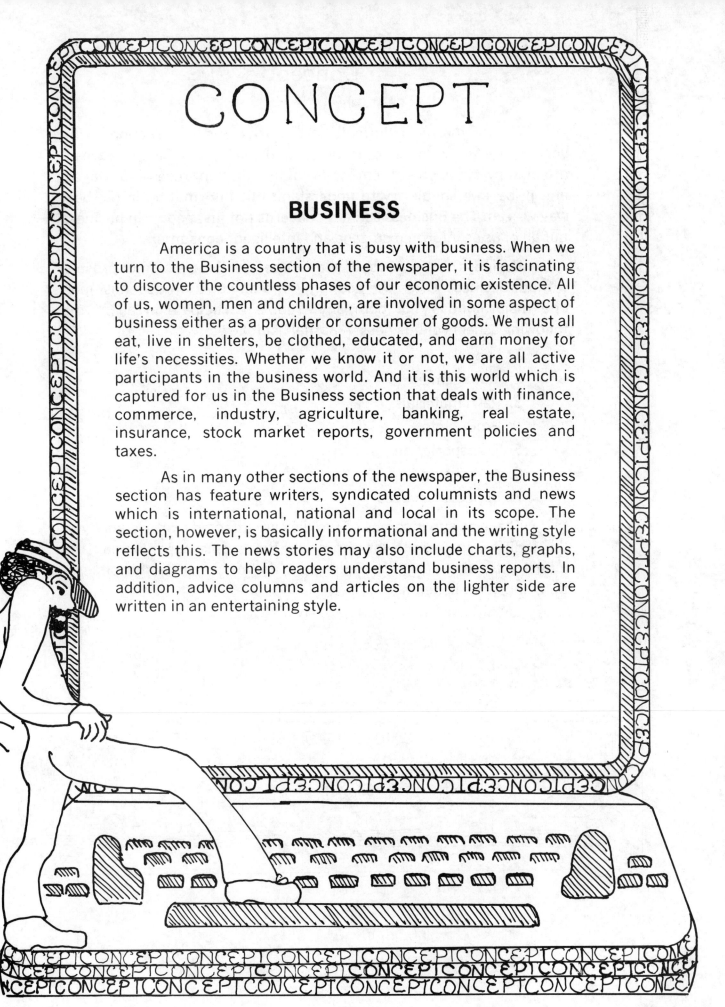

CONCEPT

BUSINESS

America is a country that is busy with business. When we turn to the Business section of the newspaper, it is fascinating to discover the countless phases of our economic existence. All of us, women, men and children, are involved in some aspect of business either as a provider or consumer of goods. We must all eat, live in shelters, be clothed, educated, and earn money for life's necessities. Whether we know it or not, we are all active participants in the business world. And it is this world which is captured for us in the Business section that deals with finance, commerce, industry, agriculture, banking, real estate, insurance, stock market reports, government policies and taxes.

As in many other sections of the newspaper, the Business section has feature writers, syndicated columnists and news which is international, national and local in its scope. The section, however, is basically informational and the writing style reflects this. The news stories may also include charts, graphs, and diagrams to help readers understand business reports. In addition, advice columns and articles on the lighter side are written in an entertaining style.

Concept

One of the most difficult parts of the Business section is the vocabulary. Many words are technical and conceptual. Since we are all affected by employment, career training, inflation, recession, wages, and prices, we should try to understand this information in the best way we can. The Business section concerns not just people in business but all of us as informed citizens and intelligent consumers.

Business cannot prosper without people. People cannot prosper without business. Often the economy of a city or town depends upon one major industry or company. People participate in all of the following aspects of business. A partial list follows:

1. Labor
2. Management
3. Raw materials
4. Production
5. Transportation
6. Advertising
7. Support services

The lives and incomes of families are affected by the stability of the industry in their towns. Primarily the people depend upon the industry for their salaries, retirement and/or pensions, hospitalization, and other benefits.

Concept

Further, this influence extends to career training and choices. It also involves support services for the population. For example: The economy of a city like Detroit, Michigan, depends on the auto industry. This includes rubber, glass and steel production, as well as warehousing, parts manufacturing factories, assembly plants, showrooms, used car lots and other related services. More than 1/3 of Detroit's 1.8 million wage earners hold jobs directly related to the auto industry. In addition, there are an infinite number of other industries that are indirectly linked to the auto business.

As industry prospers or declines, the lives of the working people are affected in their capacity to buy goods and services for their own needs.

When industry thrives, the lives of the people and the entire area flourish. Conversely, if the industry falters, then the people suffer. Employment is affected; buying power drops; the city tax base is reduced; schools, hospitals, libraries, all public institutions and municipal services suffer from a decline of revenue.

Therefore, business can be characterized as a vast network in which the proper functioning of each part is critical to the operation of all other parts. The interdependence of people and business is the heartbeat of every town and city.

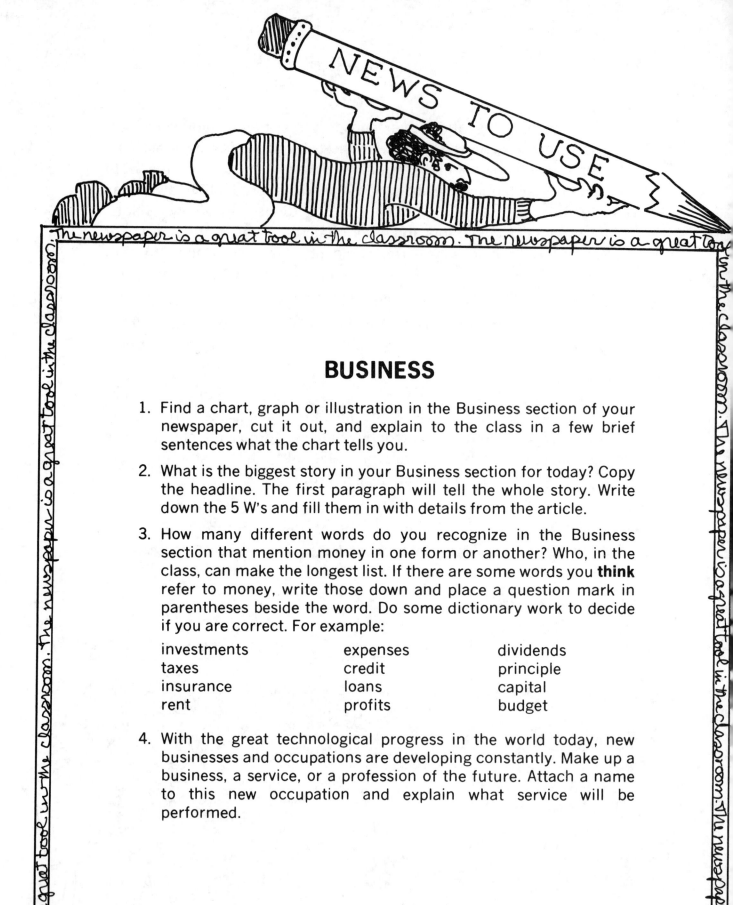

BUSINESS

1. Find a chart, graph or illustration in the Business section of your newspaper, cut it out, and explain to the class in a few brief sentences what the chart tells you.

2. What is the biggest story in your Business section for today? Copy the headline. The first paragraph will tell the whole story. Write down the 5 W's and fill them in with details from the article.

3. How many different words do you recognize in the Business section that mention money in one form or another? Who, in the class, can make the longest list. If there are some words you **think** refer to money, write those down and place a question mark in parentheses beside the word. Do some dictionary work to decide if you are correct. For example:

investments	expenses	dividends
taxes	credit	principle
insurance	loans	capital
rent	profits	budget

4. With the great technological progress in the world today, new businesses and occupations are developing constantly. Make up a business, a service, or a profession of the future. Attach a name to this new occupation and explain what service will be performed.

News to Use

5. Write to your local newspaper to get information about becoming a news carrier. Whether you are a female or a male you can qualify for this job. Having your own paper route as your first real business can be fun. List the details which are important. For example:

   a) How old must you be?
   b) What are your responsibilities?
   c) How much do the customers pay for a paper?
   d) What will the papers cost **you**?
   e) How much can you earn weekly?
   f) What hours must you work?
   g) What can you learn from this job?

6. The first homeowner on your newspaper route wants to know how much the newspapers will cost for one year. If the Sunday paper costs the customer $.50 and the daily paper costs $.20, what will the total price be for a year's delivery?

7. Scan the Business section and cut out the name of every business you can find. Describe the business. Put a question mark next to the ones you are unsure of and discuss them with the class.

News to Use

8. Find an advertisement for a bank which includes information about the interest rate that is paid to customers for their savings. If you made a savings deposit of $100 dollars, how much money would you have at the end of one year based upon your interest earnings as stated in the advertisement? (Think about compounding interest paid quarterly.) You may open your own savings account with as little as a $1.00 deposit. If possible, visit your local bank and get all the printed information you will need to open a savings account. Compare the advertisement with your local bank. Does each offer the same thing?

9. Every newspaper has its own style sheet which reporters must follow in their writing. In the Business section you will find references to large sums of money which are written out. For example: 15 million, 639 thousand, 3 hundred, etc. Find six of the largest sums in the financial section and write them out in numerals only. Can you find the style rule for your hometown newspaper concerning numbers? Look through the paper. When are digits used? When are they written out? Does your English book include this style rule? If not, find the rule elsewhere. Do the newspaper and the style book agree?

10. What businessperson would you like to meet? Perhaps you can think of a name immediately. If not, look in the Business section of your newspaper for ideas. You may select a personality who is a national figure or a businesswoman or man in your town. Print out the name of that person and pin it to your shirt. Write down on a separate sheet of paper some of your reasons for wanting to meet that person. Circulate around the room with your classmates who have made their choices as well. Stop someone who has made an interesting choice. Exchange reasons for your choice and compare.

News to Use

11. The United States and other industrial nations are in the middle of an energy crisis. This affects business in many ways. Energy is needed in four major areas:

    a. Industry
    b. Transportation
    c. Households
    d. Commercial

    We have taken our energy resources for granted and have been dangerously wasteful. We must conserve energy and begin to think about it as never before. Organize an energy bulletin board based upon the four areas above. How many newspaper articles, ads, pictures, and general items can you find in the newspaper which use or deal with energy on all four fronts? How many energy-using machines, appliances, necessities and luxuries can be listed and accounted for? How can we as private citizens help to conserve energy? Make a list of energy-saving ideas starting with your own home.

    Think hard since the obvious things may escape your attention. For example: pilot lights in stoves burn as much as 10% of all the gas used in the USA; leaky faucets waste hot water, clothes can be washed in warm or cold water; fluorescent lamps use less energy than light bulbs, etc. The following example will help you start.

ENERGY USE AT HOME	WAYS TO CONSERVE
1. Electric lights	1. Turn out lights when leaving room

    For more information on energy, write to:

    Office of Public Affairs
    Communication Services
    U.S. Department of Energy
    Washington, D.C. 20585

HOW TO READ THE STOCK MARKET TABLES

Column 1 — Start at the left. The first column **"HIGH"** tells the highest price the stock sold for **in the last year.**

Column 2 — The second column **"LOW"** tells the lowest price the stock sold for **in the last year.**

Column 3 — The third column **"STOCK"** gives the name of the company. On our chart it is ACF Industries.

Column 4 — The fourth column **"DIV"** (dividend) gives the dividend rate 2.50 which means that $2.50 a share was declared for the year. (This figure does not equal all the profit because a company must keep money to operate and grow.)

Column 5 — The fifth column **"YLD"** (yield) indicates 6.7 on our chart. This means that 6.7 percent of the price listed will be returned in dividends if all items remain the same.

Column 6 — The sixth column **"PE"** (Price Earnings Ratio) tells us on our chart that the company is earning **6** times the current price of the stock per share. For example, if you paid $10 per share, the company is earning a profit of $60 per share (6 x 10 = $60).

Column 7 — The seventh column **"100's"** means the number of shares sold that day represented in hundreds. (On our chart the number is 47). Therefore, 47 x 100 = 4700 (shares traded that day).

Column 8 — The eighth column **"HIGH"** means the highest price paid that day for that stock (on our chart 38-3/8 means $38.38).

Column 9 — The ninth column **"LOW"** means the lowest price paid that day for that stock (on our chart 37-3/8 means $37.38).

Column 10 — The tenth column **"LAST"** means the price of the last shares traded when the stock market closed at 4 p.m. in the afternoon (on our chart it is 37-3/8 or $37.38).

Column 11 — The eleventh column "CHG" (Change) means the difference expressed by plus (+) or minus (-) between today's close and yesterday's close. On our chart minus (-3/4) means the price of the stock went down 75¢ per share since yesterday. Plus (+3/4) would mean the stock went up 75¢ per share since yesterday. If there is no figure at all in the column, that means there was no change at all.

Please Note: There are other indications of items such as 1.49e which need not be explained at this time.

NEW YORK STOCK EXCHANGE
Thursday, August 28, 1980

Sales

52 WEEK

Columns:

1	2	3	4	5	6	7	8	9	10	11
High	Low	Stock	Div.	Yld.	PE	100's	High	Low	Last	Chg.
43 1/4	27 1/2	ACF	2.50	6.7	6	47	38 3/8	37 3/8	37 3/8	-3/4
20 3/4	11 1/2	AMF	1.24	6.3	7	1854	20 1/2	19 5/8	19 5/8	-5/8
22	12 1/2	AM Inti	.28	1.4	126	253	20 3/4	20 1/8	20 1/8	-3/4
12 1/4	7 7/8	APL	.50i		12	9	9 1/2	9 3/8	9 1/2	-1/8
39 3/8	24 3/4	ARA	1.94	5.4	7	58	36 1/2	35 3/4	36 1/4	-5/8
57 3/4	26 1/2	ASA	5	8.7		393	57 3/4	56 7/8	57 1/4	+1/2
15 7/8	8 1/8	ATO	.60	4.0	5	127	15 1/2	14 3/4	14 7/8	-5/8
36 3/8	17	AVX	.32	1.0	15	116	34 1/2	33 1/2	33 5/8	-1/2
51 3/4	34 1/8	AbbtLb	1.20	2.5	15	270	49 1/4	48 1/4	48 1/2	-1/2
34 1/4	18 3/4	AcmeC	1.40	4.8	6	46	29 1/4	29	29	1/2
4 3/4	2 3/4	AdmDg	.04	1.10	7	49	4	4	4	
14 7/8	11	AdaEx	1.49e	11		56	14	13 3/4	13 3/4	-1/4
7	3 5/8	AdmMl	.20e	3.2	11	131	6 3/4	6 1/8	6 1/4	-1/2
57	26 7/8	AMD n		17	279	53 3/4	52 1/4	52 1/2	-1 1/4	
39 1/2	29 1/2	AetnLF	2.12	6.1	5	313	34 3/4	34 1/2	34 1/2	
5 1/8	2	Aileen				99	5	4 7/8	5	

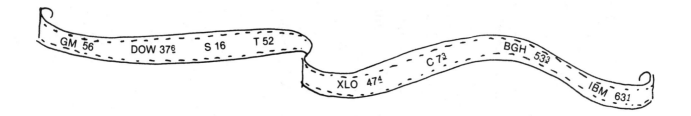

STOCK MARKET INFORMATION

For example, when you buy a share of stock of Pumpernick's Bakeries, this means you own a share of that company. You might pay 25¢ for a share and purchase an unlimited amount of shares. If the company makes a profit, they pay you money on your stock. This is called a **dividend**. If no profit is made, you do not earn a dividend. If Pumpernick's Bakeries does a lot of business, your stock is worth more when you sell it. If the business does not go well, you may want to sell your stock, but you will get less for it than what you paid.

You generally buy shares directly from a **stockbroker** who has a license. He calls the Stock Exchange to make your purchase. The American Stock Exchange (AMEX) and the New York Stock Exchange (NYSE) are both located on Wall Street, the famous financial district in New York City. At the Stock Exchange, stocks are bought and sold and the daily activity of the stock market is recorded for the country and the entire world.

The prices of stock go up and down in value. The prices are based on what someone is willing to pay for it and what the owner is willing to sell it for. People want to know whether they are making or losing money, so they watch the information in the stock tables of the daily newspaper. The following chart is a typical stock table from the newspaper which will help you follow the information, step by step. You will notice that the companies are listed alphabetically and often their names are abbreviated.

STOCK MARKET ACTIVITIES

Column:	3	8	9	10	11
COMPANY	**STOCK** (Abbreviated)	**HIGH**	**LOW**	**LAST**	**CHG**
AMERICAN AIRLINES					
AVON					
CAMPBELL SOUP					
FIRESTONE					
GENERAL MOTORS					
HERSHEY					
KRAFT					
PEPSI COLA					
PILLSBURY					
SEARS					
SUNOCO					

1. Abbreviate these ten companies according to the abbreviations which are listed on your stock market page. Use Sunday's listings as well. You may choose to select your own 11 companies and their abbreviations. Fill in the rest of the information.

2. Which stock had the highest price of the day?
   Company _____ High _____

3. Which stock had the lowest price of the day?
   Company _____ Low _____

4. What stock went up the most from the day before?
   Company _____ CHG _____

5. What stock went down the most from the day before?
   Company _____ CHG _____

6. What stock had the greatest difference in price from the "HIGH" of the day to when the stock market closed at 4 p.m.? Company _____ High _____ Last _____

7. Pick one stock as if you had purchased it as an investor. Watch the changes in the market for one or two weeks. Did you earn money, lose money, or did the stock remain the same? Write down the results.

The Big Activity

A CLASS(Y) ENTERPRISE

The best way to understand how complex business can be is to become involved in a real enterprise. Perhaps the class would like to raise money for a field trip, a class excursion, a piece of athletic equipment or for a beautiful picture to hang in the school library.

Discuss acceptable and practical ways in which the class can earn money. This may be accomplished through a bake sale, a used book sale, a Halloween pumpkin sale, a car wash, or a white elephant sale. The merchandise may be available to all the children in the school and the community. Depending on class time and curriculum needs, one or more suggested activities may be used.

The Big Activity

If the money-raising endeavor is to last all semester or for many months, several different enterprises suggested may be selected. Committees should be formed and plans for acquiring merchandise, mobilizing help and keeping financial records should be established.

Just as people in business must make the proper arrangements, permission must be granted by the school administrator to proceed. Careful record keeping and banking of the funds is required. When necessary, a cooperative parent network should be set up to assist with all the details in making the enterprise successful.

The class may design a flow chart or a mural on butcher paper with a visual description of how one or several of these profit-making enterprises would function. The mural will serve as a graphic representation of the steps the class would follow to achieve their business objective.

An evaluation of the project should be made by the class to determine its success. Suggestions for future plans can be made at this time.

IX. ADVERTISING

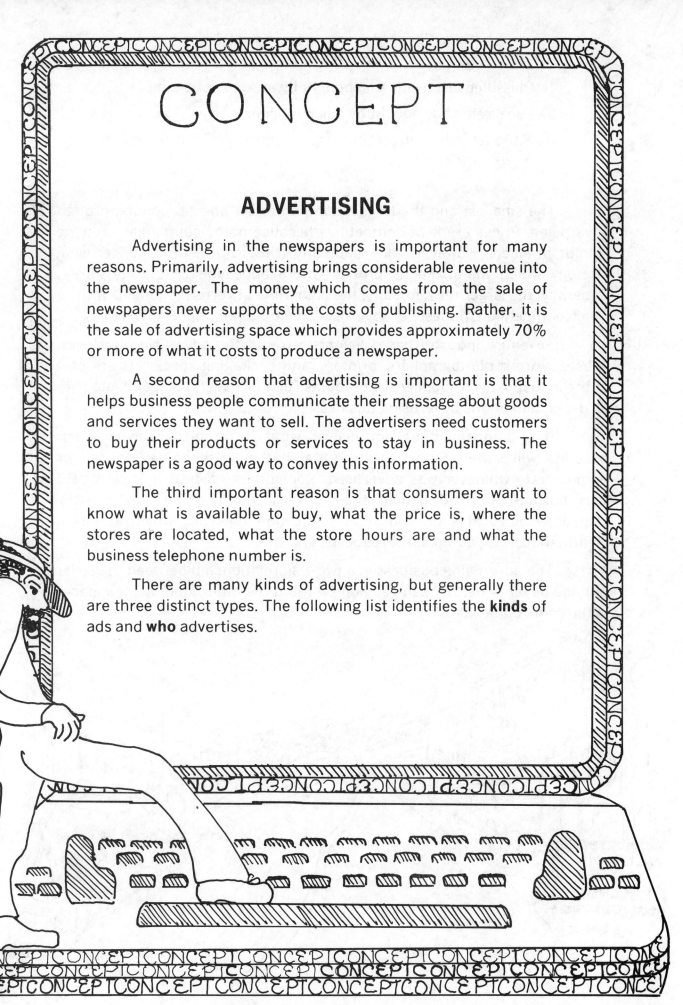

CONCEPT

ADVERTISING

Advertising in the newspapers is important for many reasons. Primarily, advertising brings considerable revenue into the newspaper. The money which comes from the sale of newspapers never supports the costs of publishing. Rather, it is the sale of advertising space which provides approximately 70% or more of what it costs to produce a newspaper.

A second reason that advertising is important is that it helps business people communicate their message about goods and services they want to sell. The advertisers need customers to buy their products or services to stay in business. The newspaper is a good way to convey this information.

The third important reason is that consumers want to know what is available to buy, what the price is, where the stores are located, what the store hours are and what the business telephone number is.

There are many kinds of advertising, but generally there are three distinct types. The following list identifies the **kinds** of ads and **who** advertises.

Concept

1. Classified ads (want ads) bought by all kinds of people.
2. Local retail ads bought by business people in your area.
3. National ads bought by large companies which advertise all across the country.

The smallest and the largest companies sell their products through advertising. Prices are kept competitive because many companies produce similar products. However, each company tries to develop an advertising strategy which will make its product more appealing to the consumer. Generally, the larger the company, the higher the advertising budget. With so much competition, honesty in advertising becomes an important issue.

An entire industry has developed around the advertising business. Artists, writers, photographers, printers, and packaging specialists are part of the industry. Even suppliers of products such as paper, ink, paint, etc., are all dependent on the advertising business.

If a company does not deliver what it promises publicly, that business will suffer. Some laws require that a business deliver, sell or demonstrate whatever was advertised. Consumers have a right to expect that businesses stand behind their advertisements. Many states have Consumer Advocates or Consumer Protection Agencies which act as a clearinghouse for complaints, requests, etc.

The advertising business is a two-way relationship between the seller and the buyer — neither can get along without the other. And the newspaper is the connecting link.

ADVERTISING

1. Pretend that a large, rich company in your town spends a lot of money advertising in your newspaper. The local government has accused the company of pouring chemical wastes into the city's river and contaminating the water. When the story breaks it is important news and you, as the editor, feature it on the front page. The president of the company is outraged when he reads the paper and threatens to withdraw all of his advertising from your paper. This is a big decision for you to make. Write him a letter regarding his threats and your decision. Role play a meeting with your editorial staff! Role play a meeting with the president of the company!

2. List some product names in the newspaper which emphasize the quality or the type of product being sold. Some brand names suggest the characteristics of the product or the job it performs. For example: IRONSIDE GLUE, PRECISION TOOLS, RADIANT SHAMPOO. Now make up some imaginative brand names for products such as:

   a. Peanut butter
   b. Deodorant
   c. Roller skates
   d. Garbage bags
   e. Cereal
   f. Hot dogs
   g. Shoe polish
   h. Sports equipment

3. Plan a party meal "from soup to nuts" for your friends. Look through the supermarket ads and cut out pictures of the items you will purchase. Paste the ads on paper. Under each picture include the description, price, quantity and the total cost of your grocery bill.

News to Use

4. Pictures of men and women are used in advertising in the newspapers and magazines all the time. Find these pictures and make lists headed, **MEN** and **WOMEN.** Write down the kinds of occupations and professions men are pictured as representing. Write down the kinds of occupations and professions women are pictured as representing. Are men always seen in particular kinds of jobs? Are women always seen in particular kinds of jobs? Are there any men's jobs pictured for which women would be qualified for as well? Who are the doctors, lawyers, ministers, mechanics, executives, athletes, politicians, etc.?

5. Write an outrageous advertisement for something that everybody can really live without. Be convincing! The "thing" you want to sell may be a product or a service. You may be a rental agency for weird pets or a manufacturer of grape peelers. Use advertising techniques you see in the paper, for example, "Look like summer all year 'round," "Visit our Bronzo Suntan Parlors," or "Prove you're a man with Macho Cologne."

News to Use

6. Are there ads for products that are bad for your health? What are these products? Are there warnings on any of the packages? Copy these warnings as they appear. Why do people use substances which they know are harmful?

7. Find an ad which you believe is not completely truthful or misleading. For example: "Lose up to 20 pounds in two weeks" — "Grow a new thick head of hair" — "Read my book and make $10 into a million." What does the ad say? Is there a possibility of exaggeration? Does it apply to everyone?

8. Reading ads in the newspaper can provide important information. Look through the food ads and write down the item, brand, amount and price. Find as many brands as possible of one item, for example, canned tomatoes. Figure out the unit price of each brand by dividing the number of ounces (oz.) into the price of the can. Sometimes the quantity is written as units. Now compare the prices and decide which brand you would buy and give at least two reasons.

News to Use

9. Write a consumer complaint to the company from which you bought something that was advertised in the newspaper. The product did not wear well, did not work or was faulty. Discuss the product as described in the ad.

10. Where would you like to spend your vacation? Find a newspaper advertisement, perhaps in the Travel section, for a trip to any place in the world. You will not have to worry about expenses. Give all the details. What form of transportation will you use? What is the fare? Who is advertising the trip? Supplement the ad by finding as much information as you can about the place you will visit. For example: What is the geographic location? How many miles is it from your city? What will the temperature be during your visit? What are the points of interest for tourists? What is the difference between the time in your city and in your vacation spot? (Eastern, Central or Mountain Time)

News to Use

11. Scan the newspaper for a "Bargain Hunt." Find advertisements for the items below. Search to find the cheapest prices. Cut out the ads to prove the accuracy of the bargains you have found. Then find a coupon for **anything** which is a big money-saving offer. Add up the five items. Then subtract the amount of that coupon from the sum of the five articles. Compare totals with everyone in the class. The least amount of money spent wins the Bargain Hunt.

Add These Prices

a. A dog . . . . _____

b. A bike . . . . _____

c. A pair of jeans . . . . _____

d. A new portable TV set . . . . . . _____

e. One pound of hamburger . . _____

                Subtotal   _____

f. Most valuable

      coupon . . . . Subtract   _____

                  TOTAL   _____

Now! Design your own Bargain Hunt based on today's paper. You may vary the math functions in any way you like.

12. Define a slogan. Write one. List some slogans or jingles from magazines and the newspaper.

13. A logo is a symbol for a business, institution or product. It is designed to attract attention and communicate immediate recognition, such as the "Golden Arches." Find as many logos as you can and cut them out for a logo bulletin board.

ART   **RESOURCES, LTD.**

BNG Associates, Inc.

Susan Solomon's
Calligraphy, Ink.

announcements
quotations
awards
menus
invitations
greeting cards
et cetera

14. Look through the newspaper to find five items you want to buy. Write out one check in payment for the five items. Design or copy a check accurately. In computing the total of five items, be sure to include sales tax when applicable.

15. Classify your ads according to what is being sold. Name the company, location and hours. For example:

Services	Manufactured Goods	Natural Resources
Restaurant	Cars	Oil

The Big Activity

CAPTURE CUSTOMERS

Divide into groups. Decide upon a company you would like to own. Find ads for similar companies in the newspaper. Look them over carefully to see the things they emphasize in order to attract customers.

You may sell **goods** (athletic equipment, pet foods, toiletries, books, records, pharmaceuticals, hardware, machinery, vehicles, — or **services** (plumbing, musical groups, carpentry, appliance or auto repair, painting, food catering).

Give your company an imaginative name. If you are selling a product, make it sound catchy. Design a logo for your business.

Think up a super advertising slogan to be used in the newspapers and on television. Write a good advertisement with a cutout picture or a cartoon you have drawn. Complete the ad with all the information the customers should have. Find out the cost of putting an ad in the daily news. What influences the cost of an advertisement?

The Big Activity

Now, each group will present a radio or TV commercial for the item they want to sell. You may sing, dance, and have props. Do all the lively things you have seen or heard which are used to sell. Convince the consumer that he/she **needs** your product! Use humor, alliteration and repetition and make your ad "good, good, good for Pizano's Perfect Pizza."

WILLIAM'S PLUMBING

"Don't take the plunge yourself. Call Willy the Plumber instead."

YAWL BROTHERS TOY STORE

"Good things come in Yawl packages."

GRANDMA ETTA'S CEREALS

"Little Miss Muffet sat on a tuffet eating Etta's oatmeal. Check it out folks. It's got curds and whey beat a mile."

ILLUSTRATIONS USED IN ADVERTISING

BIG DISCOUNTS!
YEAR ROUND
TOYS

AMERICAN MADE
BICYCLES
3-5 & 10 SPEED

SINCE 1893

TROPHIES
CUSTOM DESIGNERS

● **FABRICATORS**
● **ENGRAVERS**

SILVER ● PEWTER ● STAINLESS STEEL

★ UTILITY AWARDS
★ SALES & SERVICE AWARDS
★ PLAQUES - GAVELS & DESK SETS
★ RIBBONS ★ ROSETTES
★ CAST BRONZE & ALUMINUM PLAQUES
★ DESK SIGNS ★ BADGES ★ NAME PLATES

EL CHICO MEXICAN FOOD

ITALIAN - AMERICAN
INTERNATIONAL CUISINE
DINE-IN & CARRY OUT
4 PM TO 11 PM MON.-THUR.
4 PM TO 12 MIDNIGHT FRI· & SAT·

We're Competitive!
PLUMBING
ALTERATION
REPAIRS

NO JOB
TOO
SMALL

HOI KING LAU

HOI KING LAU...

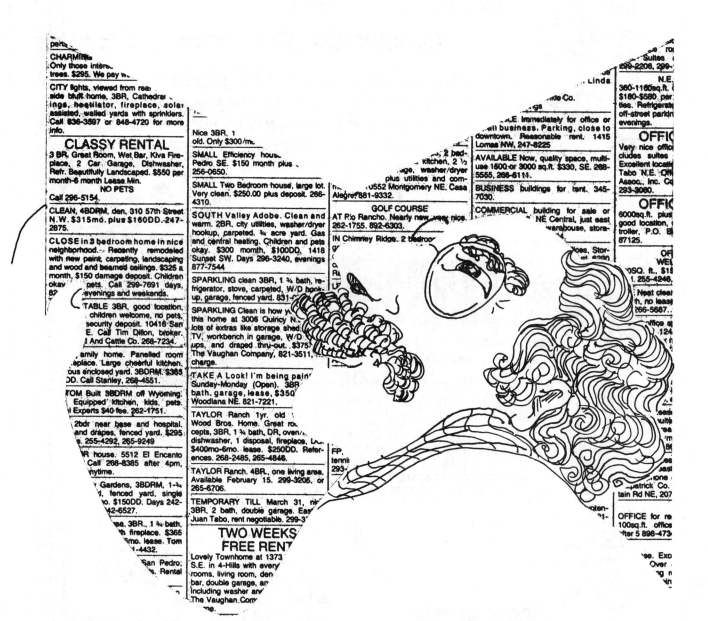

CONCEPT

CLASSIFIED ADS

The Classified Ads section is one of the most intriguing sections of the newspaper. It serves as a marketplace with its offerings of goods, services and strange information. If you want to sell your house, buy a bike, trade a refrigerator, find a family for your puppies, get a job, or locate a lost pet, look through the classified ads.

The average big city daily newspaper is jammed full of almost anything you need. The ads are divided into major sections or classifications. The major sections are broken down into smaller sections. For example: Help Wanted, a major section, will include alphabetically listed jobs from accountants to restaurant help and then become more specialized by listing **Help** — Medical — Dental — Office — Clerical or Household, etc. The Equal Employment Opportunity laws provide guidelines for what an employer can and cannot say in an advertisement.

Classified ads are written in very small print in order to accommodate the large number of ads in the least amount of space. Most of the ads are small, though businesses may choose to buy a larger ad to attract attention. Looking for a particular job or item to purchase requires time, patience and careful reading.

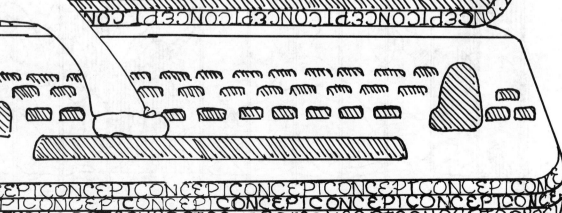

Concept

The cost of ads is determined by the number of lines and the length of the ad. The longer the ad, the more it will cost. The period of time customers want the ad to appear in the newspaper will also determine the cost. Because ads are listed alphabetically, it is a good idea to start your ad with a letter from the beginning of the alphabet. Since the information is compressed and charged by the word, it is suggested that the ad first be written out before calling it in to the Classified Ad Department. The people who answer the phones are trained to organize the customer's information in the best possible way. They will assist with suggestions and advice. They will use abbreviations to save you space — and money! The ad should get to the point and include all necessary information to attract the readers.

In responding to a classified ad, one may circle it and write out the information on a separate piece of paper for easier reading. List the phone number and major details in order to ask intelligent questions of a seller. You may have to write a letter to the person who advertised, if only a box number or an address is given in the want ad.

CLASSIFIED AD INDEX

A typical big city Classified Ad Index in the daily paper may look like this, with the most extensive ad section to be found in the Sunday edition of most papers:

The Detroit News

Michigan's Classified Leader for 53 Years!

79 OUT OF EVERY **100**

Classified Ads that ran in Detroit's two Metro Daily Newspapers appeared in The Detroit News during 1980

INDEX

The most popular classifications are listed in this index. Please refer to the Classified Pages for all classifications.

J 1 81

ANNOUNCEMENTS
Classifications 001 to 023

Death Notices ... 001
Cemeteries, Monuments ... 003
In Memoriam ... 004
Auctions ... 011
Personals, Personal Service ... 013
Attorneys, Legal Counsel ... 014
Lost & Found ... 020
Transportation, Car Pools, Travel & Tours ... 022
Legal Notices ... 023
Entertainers ... 044

EMPLOYMENT-EDUCATION
Classifications 024 to 045

Help Wanted ... 026
Help, Medical-Dental ... 027
Help, Office-Clerical ... 028
Help, Domestic ... 030
Help, Couples ... 031
Help, Sales ... 032
Situations Wanted ... 035,036,038
Educational ... 039,041

MERCHANDISE
Classifications 047 to 086

Trading Post ... 047
Sports Equipment ... 049
Diamonds, Gold, Jewelry ... 052
Miscellaneous for sale ... 054
Flea Markets, Garage & Rummage Sales ... 055
Cameras & Supplies ... 058
Bicycles ... 061
Office Equip., Computers ... 062
Restaurant Equipment ... 064
Antiques, Collectibles ... 066
Appliances ... 067
Furniture, Lamps, Rugs ... 070
Home Furnishings ... 074
Moving, Storage & Mini-Storage ... 075
Stereo-Hi Fi, etc. ... 078
Television ... 079
Musical Instruments ... 080
Pianos, Organs ... 081
Building Materials ... 083
Machinery & Supplies ... 086

TRANSPORTATION
Classifications 088 to 133

Autos for Sale ... 084 to 116
Trucks, Trailers ... 118
Vans, Accessories ... 119
Tires, Auto Accessories, Salvage ... 120
Recreation Vehicles ... 126
Aircraft & Air Freight ... 128
Motorcycles, Mopeds & Mini-Bikes ... 129
Boats, Motors ... 130
Sailboats ... 131
Performance Boats, Access. ... 132
Snowmobiles, All Terrain Vehicles ... 133

BUSINESS SERVICES
Classifications 172 to 228

PETS
Classifications 231 to 240

Horses, Livestock, Equip. ... 231
Pets-General ... 232
Tropical Fish & Accessories ... 233
Cats ... 236
Dogs, Kennels ... 238

REAL ESTATE
Classifications 259 to 304

Real Estate Outside Detroit ... 269
Lake, River Property ... 271
Florida Property, Sell-Buy-Rent-Lease ... 273
Acreage, Sell-Buy ... 276
Comm. Bldgs., Land ... 280, 281
Ind'l Bldgs., Land ... 281, 284
Houses, East & West ... 289, 291
Condominiums, Co-ops ... 292
Houses, Suburban East ... 294
Houses, Suburban West ... 295
Mobile Homes ... 304

RENTALS
Classifications 306 to 333

Houses to Rent, East ... 308
Houses to Rent, West ... 309
Flats, Furnished-Unfurn. ... 314
Apartments, Suburban ... 315
Apartments, East ... 316
Apartments, West ... 317
Apartments, Furnished ... 321
Rooms ... 326
Office Space ... 330

BUSINESS OPPORTUNITIES
Classifications 334 to 342

Business Opps, General ... 335
Franchise ... 336
Bars, Beer & Wine ... 337
Drug Stores, Pharmacies ... 338
Gas Stations, Garages ... 339
Groceries & Meats ... 340
Hotels, Motels, Resorts ... 341
Restaurants ... 342

Permission of *The Detroit News*, Detroit, Michigan, 1981.

A look into the Classified Ad section reveals mystery, sadness, humor, romance and commentary on the human condition. This colorful aspect should not be neglected if the full dimension of these ads is to be appreciated!

CLASSIFIED ADS

1. Look at the Classified Ad Index of your newspaper for a fuller understanding of all categories which are included. By referring to the index, the most popular items can usually be found by category and page number. If there is something which is not included you must then look in the actual ads for a more specific item. A typical index has major headings with items grouped under them. Some major headings could be:

**ANNOUNCEMENTS   EMPLOYMENT
MERCHANDISE   TRANSPORTATION
REAL ESTATE   RENTALS   BUSINESS OPPORTUNITIES**

Use the index to find the following information. Give the major heading and the page number.

EXAMPLE   **HEADING   PAGE**

a. Your brother wants to buy a new van.   _____ ____

b. Your mother needs an attorney to look at
   a contract.   _____ ____

c. Your sister wants a job as an auto
   mechanic.   _____ ____

d. Where can your teacher find a used
   camera?   _____ ____

e. The church needs a new organ.   _____ ____

f. The family wants to rent a house.   _____ ____

g. Your grandparents want to buy a
   mobile home.   _____ ____

h. Uncle Jim wants to buy a gas station.   _____ ____

News to Use

2. Remember that all ads must include important information and be understandable. Write out an ad for each of the following:

   a. Sell your bike
   b. Advertise for something you lost
   c. Advertise a rummage sale in your garage

   If you prefer, you may advertise anything of your choice. Include your phone number, price and the condition of the item, etc.

3. Look under **Real Estate**. Find the home, cottage or cabin of your choice. Cut out the ad and describe it in a written paragraph or orally to the class. You may want to fill in even more information than what was included in the ad. Be creative.

4. Look under **Transportation**. Find the car, motorcycle or minibike of your dreams. What is the cost and how long will it take you to pay for it? Make up your own weekly salary and then determine what your payments will be.

News to Use

5. Countless different careers and professions are mentioned in the classified ads such as a millwright, cost analyst, marine engineer, computer programmer, dog groomer, restaurateur, lawn doctor, certified public accountant, etc. Using the classified ads find the names of careers you have never heard of before or those about which you know very little. Do some research to find out what these careers are.

6. Look under the **Announcements** or use the index to find the death notices. List the ages of the deceased people. Figure out the average age of the people listed. What is the difference between death notices and obituaries?

7. Look in the **Announcements** and find Personal Services. Find an ad that you think is strange or interesting. For example: "Hypnosis in your home or office — Over 50 programs — Control smoking and appetite — 24-hour service — 7 days" or "Let Bongo the Gorilla sing a happy birthday greeting to your friend, in person."

8. Look under **Business Opportunities**. Describe the business you would like to buy. Give the price and all other available information as well as terms of purchase. Give the reasons you would like to own that particular type of business.

News to Use

9. Find 10 very intriguing items you would like to buy in the **Merchandise** column, such as an organ, ice-cream machine, airplane, etc. Make a list of them and choose one item that would please you!

10. Is there something in the **Lost and Found** section or **Personals** which you cannot believe? Does it suggest a story to you? Fill in the details with your own imagination and write "The Story Behind the Want Ad."

11. Ads are placed in each section of the Want Ads in alphabetical order. Sometimes you want your ad to be the first to attract attention so you might start this way: "**An a**bsolutely **a**stonishing **b**argain!" Try this technique yourself with something you want to sell.

12. Put X's on jobs in the ads which state that they require a high school diploma. Circle ads for jobs which you think require special training.

13. You will notice that the ads contain many abbreviations which help shorten the length of the ad. If the abbreviations stand alone it can be difficult to figure out what they mean. Because the shortened words are in a particular kind of category, **Housing** and **Help Wanted**, it is possible to figure out the word that has been shortened. Find about 10 of these with your classmates. Exchange the abbreviations with each other. Use no clues and see how well you translate the abbreviations. For example:

Abbreviation	Word	Abbreviation	Word
refs	references	furn'd	furnished
trans	transportation	bsmt	basement
clk	clerk	rms	rooms
incl	included	opr	operator
exp	experienced	secy	secretary
bus	business	utils	utilities
mo	month	frplc	fireplace
ofc	office	gar	garage
req'd	required	condo	condominium

News to Use

14. An ad in the Classified section costs $7.50 with 30 characters for each line. Calculate the cost of an ad that contains 90 characters. What is the cost for 100 characters? Use this form to send your ad into the Classified section.

The Westwood Banner

Use this coupon to place your ad TODAY!
Get into the want ad habit.

The first line is only 24 characters including space (the first two words are capitalized). All remaining lines are 30 characters.

Please start my ad _____

Check enclosed ☐   Bill me ☐

Name _____   Phone _____

Address _____   City _____ Zip _____

The Big Activity

GET THAT JOB

1. As a class, read some jobs from the Help Wanted section. Discuss the qualifications, salary, etc.

2. Discuss the limitations of age, lack of training, and experience, etc., when looking for employment.

3. Make conclusions about the qualifications generally required, that is, special training, high school diploma and experience.

The Big Activity

4. Discuss a job hunt on two levels. On a realistic level, what could you do at this point in your life to earn money? On a fantasy level, as an adult what would you like to be? What do you see ahead for yourself in a career?

5. If you have a particular vocation or profession in mind, research the education and kind of training which is required to qualify for that job. How much money do you think a person in that job earns?

6. Study examples of a proper business letter. Discuss the parts of the letter in detail before each class member writes to apply for a job advertised in the Help Wanted section.

7. Write a letter of application expressing your interest in a job you have found in the classified ads. The letter you are writing represents you to an interested employer who will read it and may hire you. The following guide includes all the information you need. Your letter may be real or may reflect a desire for a particular kind of employment in the future.

The Big Activity

(Your Address)
490 Evergreen Road
Jasper Heights, MI 48238
(Date) Sept. 12, 19___

(Addressee)
Ms. Helen Mandy
Yesterday's Books
2001 Greenfield Road
Oakwood, MI 48237

(Salutation)
Dear Ms. Mandy:

　　(Body of letter)

1. The name and date of the newspaper in which you read the ad.
2. The job for which you are applying.
3. Your qualifications and age.
4. Your job experience (news carrier, baby-sitter, clerk, etc.) or make up experience you think would qualify you for this job.
5. The name of a person who will provide a character reference.
6. Your phone number and when you can be reached.

(Complimentary close)
Sincerely yours,

(Signature)

7. Don't forget to address an envelope, too!

Your Name and Address

stamp

Addressee

XI. ENTERTAINMENT AND LEISURE

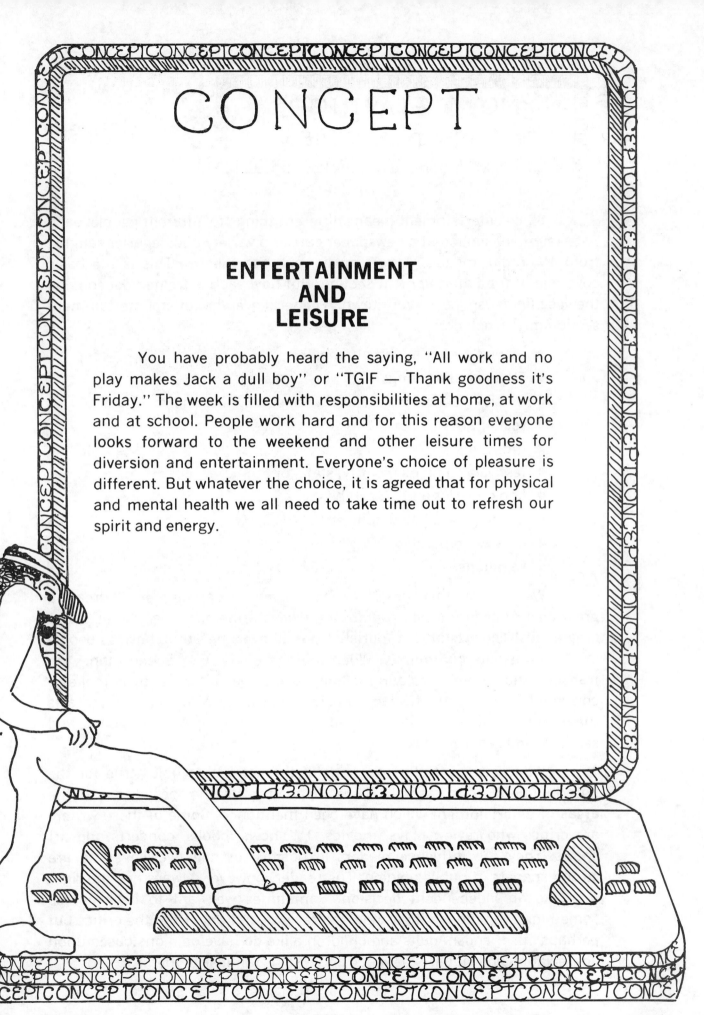

CONCEPT

ENTERTAINMENT AND LEISURE

You have probably heard the saying, "All work and no play makes Jack a dull boy" or "TGIF — Thank goodness it's Friday." The week is filled with responsibilities at home, at work and at school. People work hard and for this reason everyone looks forward to the weekend and other leisure times for diversion and entertainment. Everyone's choice of pleasure is different. But whatever the choice, it is agreed that for physical and mental health we all need to take time out to refresh our spirit and energy.

NOW PLAYING
THE GOOD APPLE REVIEW

Concept

Since entertainment means different things to different people, each Entertainment section of a newspaper carries a variety of categories ranging from TV, radio, movies, dance, music, and the theatre. This is the basic coverage of the Entertainment section. But **how** each is treated depends on the specific newspaper in your town. A general overview of an Entertainment section might include:

- movies and/or legitimate theatre
- TV and radio listings
- music — concerts — records, (classical, pop and rock)
- restaurants
- museums
- festivals and fairs (county, state, or ethnic)
- book reviews and art exhibits
- dance (disco, ballet, folk, etc.)
- crossword puzzles
- vacations

We all know that the arts — theatre, music, painting, etc. — create a great deal of beauty in life. We do not always remember that the arts also create jobs! The arts attract tourists from all over the world, besides people in the immediate community. When tourists travel, they spend money on transportation, hotels, restaurants and stores. The cultural activity makes a community more attractive to industry. One must also think of the arts themselves as a major industry which employs people, uses goods and services, and generates taxes.

What is true of other sections of the newspaper holds true for the Entertainment section as well. There are columnists who specialize in all the areas of entertainment which have been mentioned. Some of these writers are critics who review plays, movies, TV shows, books, concerts and art shows. They can influence readers in positive or negative ways and are strong shapers of public opinion. The reader, however, always has the right to make an independent decision. Sometimes we want to hear or see something even though it has had bad reviews, not only from the critics but perhaps our friends. Adults and children alike **do** have opinions based upon appreciation, individual experience and what is familiar to them.

Concept

We may not have technical knowledge or expertise — but as in all things it need not stand in the way of appreciation. Intellectual honesty is worth striving toward. Though the whole world may acclaim a painting, a piece of music or a performance, it may not inspire or excite us. Conversely, if we respond in spirit we are not obliged to give reasons why. Too much analysis may be the enemy of true appreciation. We must always, however, strive to learn more!

A feature story about a famous celebrity may also appear in this section. Generally, it is an interview and would be considered straight entertaining writing. The reporter can combine fact with analysis and opinion — sometimes humorous and caustic. The reporter has an opportunity to write persuasively in this section too!

So dip into the articles, announcements and advertisements in the Entertainment section and see what is there for you! Be open and don't be afraid to chance something new in **your** search for leisure-time activities. Your Friday or Sunday paper may have the most complete entertainment coverage of the week.

ENTERTAINMENT AND LEISURE

1. Here are some words you may find in the Entertainment section of your newspaper. Find their definitions in the dictionary and use the words in your own sentences. You may find other unfamiliar words to define for this lesson.

audio	abstract painting
encore	percussion
playwright	adapted
debut	sculptor
premiere	conductor
maestro	sculpture
TV pilot	mime
repertoire	medium (art)
acoustics	preview
choreography	musical score
soloist	AM/FM radio
cast	flick

PBS Public Broadcasting System

2. Cut out a dramatic picture from an Entertainment section. Paste it on paper and explain what you think it is about. An advertisement for a horror movie is good for this assignment.

News to Use

3. Look in the TV listings of your newspaper. There, you will find descriptions of story lines for that day. Expand the story line of four programs in any way that makes it interesting. Introduce new characters to thicken the plot. For example:

Channel 13
"The Phantom Cargo,"
1979, Yosel Boucansky,
Marvin Lawrence,
Sherry Campbell.
Cargo plane crashes
and giant ants
troop off
with all the
luggage.

Channel 9
"Exotic Space Trip,"
1969, Rube Weiss,
Gabriel Bolkosky,
Geraldine Natalie.
A futuristic sorcerer
plans to attack the de-
fenseless planet Earth by
contaminating the water
with a laughing potion.

Channel 50 Jungle Movie
"The Supreme,
Women," 1975,
Donna Watson,Karen
Haydu, Nancy John.
Slave traders travel
deep into the rain
forest to find an advanced
society led by mag-
nificent women.

Channel 20 Thriller Movie
"Curse of the
Slime Monster,"
Adam Lenter, Alfie
Blain, Hortense Farfel.
Young oceanographer
meets a mad
scientist who creates
a new grotesque
form of sea life.

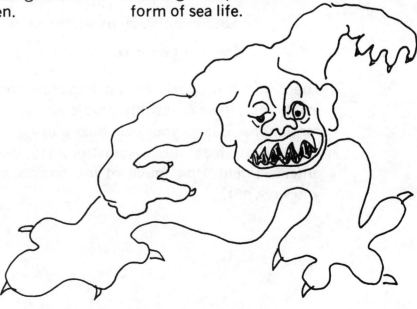

News to Use

4. Conduct a press conference where several students act as reporters and one person is a celebrity. Decide who the celebrity will be. Have each reporter prepare three interesting questions before coming to the press conference. Make sure the questions and answers will be informative and of general interest to the reading public. You may want to tape-record this interview!

5. Find the name and location of a restaurant where you would like to eat dinner. How much do you think it would cost? How could you find out ahead of time? Find the names of some ethnic restaurants in the newspapers. List them according to their nationality group, such as Italian, Mexican, Chinese, Hungarian, etc. What specialty dish would you order at each of these ethnic restaurants?

6. Look in the Movie section to find out how the movies are rated. Discuss the purpose and value of the ratings. What do the following mean?

RATING	ANSWERS
G —	All ages admitted, General Audience
PG —	All ages admitted, Parental Guidance suggested
R —	Restricted, Persons under 18 not admitted unless accompanied by parent or adult
X —	Persons under 18 not admitted

7. The crossword puzzle in the Entertainment section has many loyal fans. Find a crossword puzzle and study it carefully. Using it for a model, design your own puzzle using a piece of graph paper. Use words that have something to do with the field of entertainment. How much of the original crossword puzzle can you work out?

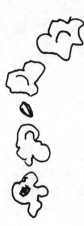

8. Find the section which describes new recordings that are at the top of the charts. List those which you would like to own. What are the titles and names of the recording artists? What are the names of the recording companies which produced the records?

9. What is the name of the music critic who represents your newspaper? Has the critic reviewed a classical, rock, pop, or jazz performance? Write in your own words how this person felt about the performance which was reviewed. Underline the facts in the article. Underline what sounds to you like opinion.

10. Are there advertisements in your paper for legitimate theatre productions where live actors and actresses perform on stage? What are the titles of these productions? Include school, church and community house plays and musicals. How much does a ticket cost? Is it more than admission to a movie?

News to Use

11. Determine the day on which your newspaper features book reviews (probably in the Sunday edition). Find a book review that makes the book sound interesting, informative, funny, or sad. Tell the class about it giving your reasons for choosing that book as one you'd like to read. Try to write a review of a book that you have read. Did you enjoy it? Did you dislike it? Why?

12. Find a movie review of a film you have seen or would like to see. What details does the critic use to describe the movie? For example: Was the acting convincing? Was the story exciting or boring? Was it in a modern or historical setting? Why do you think a critic or reviewer never tells the reader about the ending of a book, play or movie? Give your reasons. Write your own review of a movie you have seen — good or bad!

13. Pretend that you are given the job of writing the publicity for an art show in your school or community. How much will the admission be? Is there an art museum in your community or nearby? What information would you include in an advertisement that would attract museum visitors? What art media will be included: watercolors, pen and ink sketches, oil paintings, sculpture, ceramics, photography, and other crafts? Will this art be original? What is the difference between an original and a reproduction?

14. Find a listing for a movie theatre which is featuring a movie you want to see. Write down the address and phone number of the theatre. Call to find out how much the admission will be for you and your family? What is the time schedule for the movie for the entire evening? Are there any matinee performances? What is the price? Compare day and evening rates.

The Big Activity

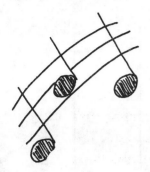
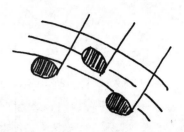

GOOD TIMES CALENDAR

Design an Entertainment and Leisure Guide which includes events in music, dance, theatre, art and cinema in your town or nearby communities. List the event, time, date, place and cost of admission. Examine your newspaper carefully for announcements of these activities. Is there a particular day of the week when the most complete listing of these events is featured in your newspaper?

Use the Good Times Calendar on the following page to organize your entertainment plans for the week.

GOOD TIMES CALENDAR

	DATE	TIME	PLACE	EVENT	COST
SUNDAY					
MONDAY					
TUESDAY					
WEDNESDAY					
THURSDAY					
FRIDAY					
SATURDAY					

What would you choose to do with a friend on any one day, if you had all the money you needed?

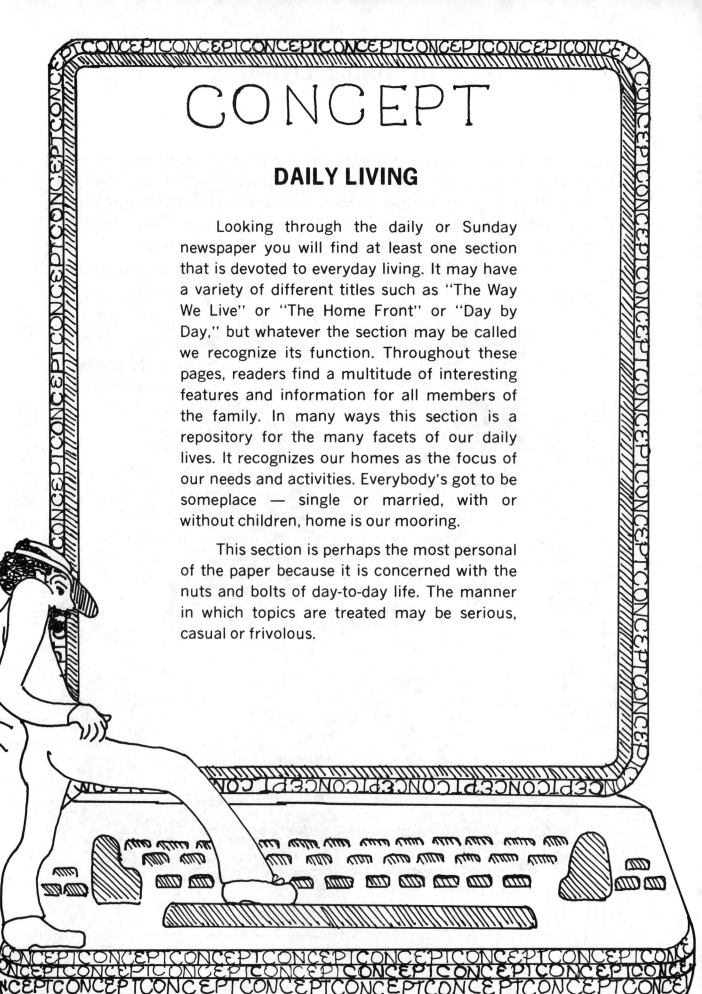

CONCEPT

DAILY LIVING

Looking through the daily or Sunday newspaper you will find at least one section that is devoted to everyday living. It may have a variety of different titles such as "The Way We Live" or "The Home Front" or "Day by Day," but whatever the section may be called we recognize its function. Throughout these pages, readers find a multitude of interesting features and information for all members of the family. In many ways this section is a repository for the many facets of our daily lives. It recognizes our homes as the focus of our needs and activities. Everybody's got to be someplace — single or married, with or without children, home is our mooring.

This section is perhaps the most personal of the paper because it is concerned with the nuts and bolts of day-to-day life. The manner in which topics are treated may be serious, casual or frivolous.

Concept

When we consider a household we think of guidelines for cooperative living, shared responsibilities, values to live by, role models and sex roles. Further we must regard households as having a tremendous impact on the marketplace because of diversified interests, varying life-styles and the need for goods and services.

If one were to make just a **partial** list of popular topics to be found in a Daily Living section, it would look something like this:

1. home improvement
2. fashions
3. decorating
4. travel
5. food
6. consumer tips
7. gossip
8. health care
9. lawn and garden care
10. pet care
11. sewing tips
12. complaint columns
13. do-it-yourself tips
14. coupons
15. horoscope
16. education
17. energy savers
18. advice (child, teen-age, adult)

Here, once again, may be found the three writing styles — informative, entertaining and persuasive. Because of its diverse readership, this section contains the greatest variety of content and writing styles.

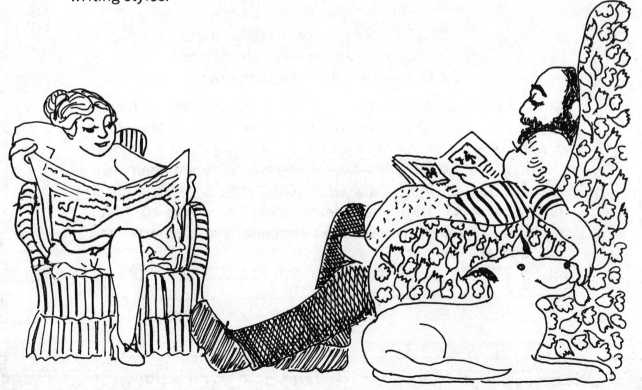

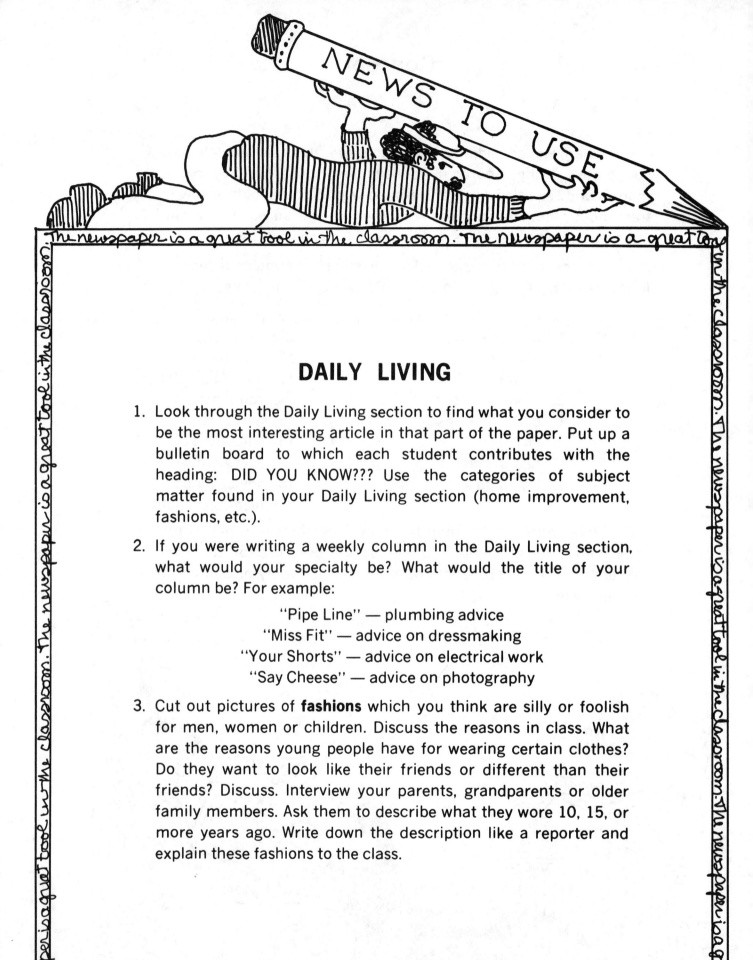

DAILY LIVING

1. Look through the Daily Living section to find what you consider to be the most interesting article in that part of the paper. Put up a bulletin board to which each student contributes with the heading: DID YOU KNOW??? Use the categories of subject matter found in your Daily Living section (home improvement, fashions, etc.).

2. If you were writing a weekly column in the Daily Living section, what would your specialty be? What would the title of your column be? For example:

    "Pipe Line" — plumbing advice
    "Miss Fit" — advice on dressmaking
    "Your Shorts" — advice on electrical work
    "Say Cheese" — advice on photography

3. Cut out pictures of **fashions** which you think are silly or foolish for men, women or children. Discuss the reasons in class. What are the reasons young people have for wearing certain clothes? Do they want to look like their friends or different than their friends? Discuss. Interview your parents, grandparents or older family members. Ask them to describe what they wore 10, 15, or more years ago. Write down the description like a reporter and explain these fashions to the class.

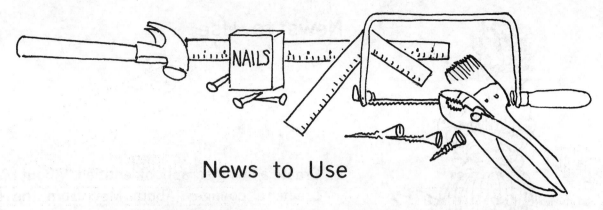

News to Use

4. Look in the **horoscope** section and find your sign. Keep track of the predictions daily for one week. Did any of them come true? Explain why you do or do not believe in horoscopes. Look in the dictionary to find the difference between astrology and astronomy.

5. Clip grocery **coupons** in one issue of your daily newspaper. List the items and the money you would save if you use the coupons. Compare your savings with others in your class. What is the largest sum of money you would save? How many things advertised in the coupons could be used in your house or could be used for food? Do you really need these items? Discuss the purpose and influence of coupons.

6. Find a **recipe** which you think would really be delicious. Write out the recipe and double it. Write out the abbreviations making sure you know what they stand for, for example, tbsp., lb., tsp., oz., c., pt., etc.

7. Find a **do-it-yourself tip** in the Daily Living section that you think could be used in your house. Take it home to whoever is the mechanic in your family and ask them to give you a mechanical "helpful hint" to report back to the class.

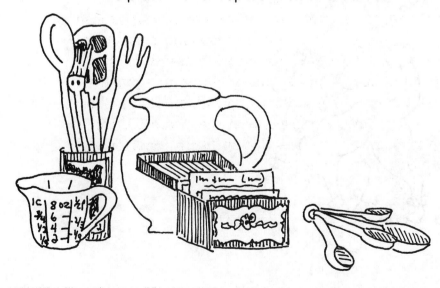

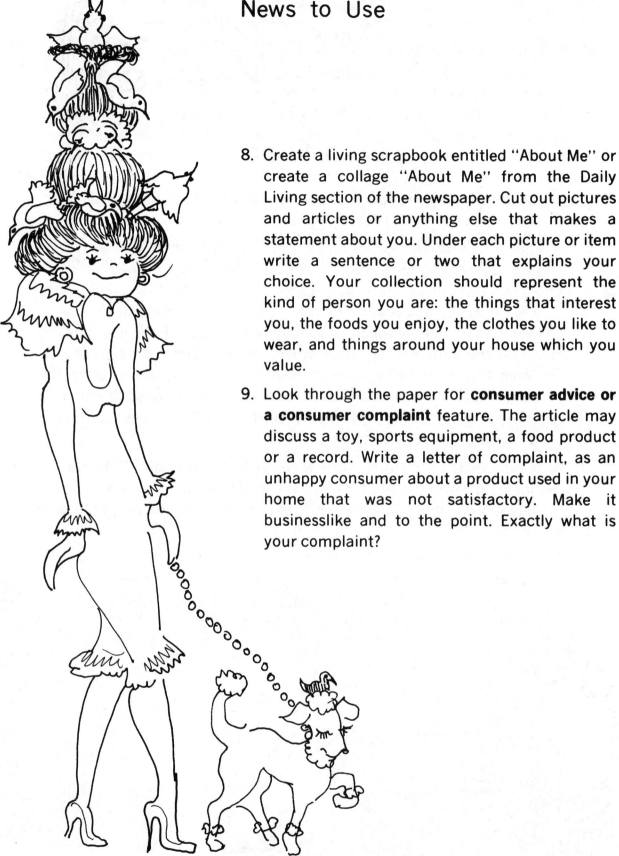

8. Create a living scrapbook entitled "About Me" or create a collage "About Me" from the Daily Living section of the newspaper. Cut out pictures and articles or anything else that makes a statement about you. Under each picture or item write a sentence or two that explains your choice. Your collection should represent the kind of person you are: the things that interest you, the foods you enjoy, the clothes you like to wear, and things around your house which you value.

9. Look through the paper for **consumer advice or a consumer complaint** feature. The article may discuss a toy, sports equipment, a food product or a record. Write a letter of complaint, as an unhappy consumer about a product used in your home that was not satisfactory. Make it businesslike and to the point. Exactly what is your complaint?

News to Use

10. **Dream Home.** Find an advertisement for a new home which includes the floor plan with area dimensions of each room. Using this as a model, use graph paper to design your own dream house. Increase or decrease the size of the rooms. Add any other rooms you would like to have in your dream house. Add a swimming pool, basketball court or anything else which pleases you. Multiply the length times the width of the house and you will get the total area of the house. Is the architecture of the house described as modern, ranch, Tudor, colonial, bungalow, Cape Cod, tri-level or other?

11. Is there an **advice column** for children or teen-agers in your newspaper? What is its name? What is the name of an advice column for grown-ups? Children, like adults, have problems which trouble them. Ask each student to write an unsigned letter describing a problem. Read the letters in class and have a discussion about how each problem may be solved. Is there more than one solution? Are there problems which are common and shared by others about friends? popularity? allowances? parents? etc.?

12. Make a demonstration speech about a special interest you have that you would like to share with the class. Think about hobbies, your favorite entertainment, a family activity which you enjoy. Prepare a demonstration presentation which will explain clearly to others what this spare time interest is. Make a written plan for yourself and prepare any props which you might need to make the demonstration come alive.

127

JUNK FOOD HALL OF FAME

Some of us eat to live and some of us live to eat! No matter which kind of person we are, we all must eat. There is a strong need for children and adults to develop "food awareness," because of all the processed foods that are on the market today. The term junk food describes those foods which can be fun to eat, are easily available, but are **not** always nutritious and are generally full of empty calories.

Health experts now believe that the public should be most concerned about the amount of **fat, sugar,** and **salt** (and food additives) we ingest. Of course, the amount of caloric intake is also a major concern. Specialists, who are interested in good nutrition, are learning that many serious diseases are related to the over-indulgence of foods which are heavy in fat, sugar and salt content.

The Big Activity

On all cans and packages of food there are labels which indicate the natural ingredients and the many chemical additives that are in the product. But that sounds simpler than what it is because, in fact, labels are really hard to read and understand. First, they are printed in very small type and second, one must almost have to be a chemist to understand what those ingredients are.

Because the last significant food labeling law was passed in 1938, three federal agencies are banding together to change the entire labeling system on foods. These agencies are the Food and Drug Administration (FDA), the Department of Agriculture (USDA), and the Federal Trade Commission (FTC). These agencies want consumers to know what is in the food products they eat.

There are 1700 natural and synthetic flavors used in food today, but the current law requires only that these be called "flavoring." Some food coloring and food preservatives (nitrates and nitrites) are also a source of concern to nutritionists, since they are sometimes considered dangerous and are used widely.

The labels on most processed foods must list ingredients in the descending order of concentration and weight. The first three ingredients on a label are the predominant ones in the product. If a label reads vegetable oil, modified corn starch and lactose milk sugar, that means the main ingredient is oil, the second ingredient in a lesser amount is cornstarch, and the third ingredient in an even lesser amount is a form of sugar.

It is interesting to note that there is much **hidden** sugar in food products which go under the various names of dextrose, honey, corn syrup, corn sweetener, molasses, invert sugar, etc. It would be easier for consumers to understand if a label simply stated what percentage of that package food is sugar, such as "Tillie's Breakfast Treats — 50% sugar."

The Big Activity

Nutritional information, by law, must be stated on a label in a particular order:

1. Size of serving

2. Servings per package

3. Calories per serving

4. Grams of protein

5. Carbohydrates and fat

6. Percentages of Recommended Daily Allowances (RDA) for protein, vitamins A and C, thiamine, riboflavin, niacin, calcium and iron, in that order

This information is only the beginning of a project bulletin board entitled, "THE JUNK FOOD HALL OF FAME." Start by doing some research in the school library. Pay special attention to the dates of the books and magazines which you use, since so much new information is available. Find out what the following additives are:

red food coloring	ascorbic acid
dextrose	sodium nitrite
modified food starch	soybean oil
whey powder	carob powder
natural flavoring	caramel color
citric acid	disodium quanylate
corn syrup	sodium silicoaluminate

Now, add to your list whatever new chemicals you notice as listed on labels.

The Big Activity

Cut out articles from the newspaper which deal with the subject of natural and processed foods. Follow up with pictures from supermarket ads of foods which are related to the articles to be attached to the bulletin board. Bring in labels from home to examine and consider for the class display. In your readings of labels, take note of the company address of the food manufacturer. Write for more information about the ingredients in their product. You will probably receive an answer. Display your letters and the responses from the food companies.

For contrast, exhibit labels and packages from natural, nourishing foods. After acquiring information from your library or research work, the class may want to send home a newsletter entitled "DO YOU KNOW WHAT YOUR CHILDREN ARE EATING?"

Books like *Eater's Digest*, by Michael Jacobson, will explain many additive terms. The Food and Drug Administration and the Department of Agriculture are good sources of nutrition information. At the end of this project you will understand more about what you and your family members eat. Work toward being a more intelligent consumer!

XIII. THE CLASS NEWSPAPER

THE CLASS NEWSPAPER

Special Note to the Teacher

This section is a culminating experience designed to achieve several objectives:

1. As a guide for the actual production of a class newspaper.

2. As an aid to reinforce the concepts in the book.

3. As a way to enhance understanding by "doing."

Because of time limitations or other constraints, it may not be possible to publish a class newspaper. In that event, the teacher may select activities from this section to emphasize those concepts which have particular significance for the class.

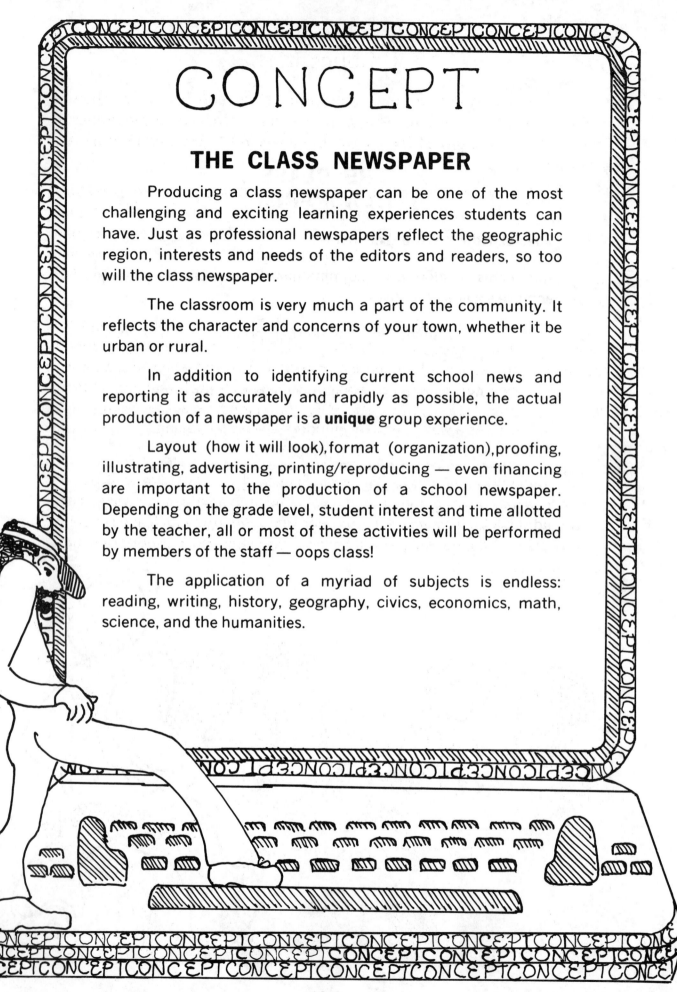

CONCEPT

THE CLASS NEWSPAPER

Producing a class newspaper can be one of the most challenging and exciting learning experiences students can have. Just as professional newspapers reflect the geographic region, interests and needs of the editors and readers, so too will the class newspaper.

The classroom is very much a part of the community. It reflects the character and concerns of your town, whether it be urban or rural.

In addition to identifying current school news and reporting it as accurately and rapidly as possible, the actual production of a newspaper is a **unique** group experience.

Layout (how it will look), format (organization), proofing, illustrating, advertising, printing/reproducing — even financing are important to the production of a school newspaper. Depending on the grade level, student interest and time allotted by the teacher, all or most of these activities will be performed by members of the staff — oops class!

The application of a myriad of subjects is endless: reading, writing, history, geography, civics, economics, math, science, and the humanities.

Concept

The opportunity to motivate individual students with a variation of skills and abilities is obvious. The value of working cooperatively in groups to meet a deadline is one of the paramount goals in the production of a class newspaper.

Almost every class has the makings of a newspaper staff — editors, writers, reporters, artists/photographers, business managers — and even newspaper carriers! This is the opportunity for students to **discover** new abilities, **refine** established skills, and **interact** with others in a new and productive manner. Here you have the "heart" and purpose for producing your own newspaper.

Developing a class newspaper emphasizes basic skills through the reportage of activities in the school, the home and the neighborhood. Because of the variety of students and outside interests, the newspaper will assume its own personality and style. Indeed, it will reach and appeal to an "audience" that perhaps has never fully understood a newspaper. Just as a local newspaper appeals to people with varied interests, so may your classroom paper be of interest to other grades.

In-depth exposure to the newspaper as a practical life skill has an immediate goal and a long-range goal. The immediate goals have been identified. As a long-range goal, consider that after students leave school, it is possible that the newspaper will become the single most important source of adult reading.

Concept

PRODUCTION GUIDE FOR A CLASS NEWSPAPER

The following chart describes the jobs to be assigned to students in the production of a class newspaper, with the related newspaper terminology beside each task.

JOB DESCRIPTION

STUDENT JOBS	PROFESSIONAL TITLE
Gathering and writing the news	Reporters
Editing the news for good taste, factual and grammatical errors, and writing headlines	Copy Editor
Designing and organizing sections of the newspaper	Format Person
Arranging position of articles	Layout/Makeup Person
Drawing or taking pictures	Illustrator or Photographer
Selling space to describe goods and services	Advertising Person
Typing, hand printing, reproducing or duplicating	Production Person
Delivering newspaper	Circulation Person

Concept

The production of the newspaper can be a culminating activity, where students demonstrate a new understanding of how a newspaper is put together. Even a single, quality issue will be enough to meet the goal of cognitive growth. Here as always, process is more important than product — how and what the students learn together is more important than the actual newspaper they produce.

Some Basic Suggestions Prior to Production:

1. What should be included in our newspaper—human interest, school events, letters to the editor, interviews?

2. How many jobs must be filled—reporters, editors, illustrators?

3. Who will perform the jobs?

4. Will groups or individuals be assigned tasks?

5. What will the size and format of the newspaper be?

6. How long will it take to produce the newspaper—starting and deadline dates?

7. What are some general rules we should establish for this cooperative project?

Concept

8. Will there be a specific time set aside each day for working on the newspaper?

9. How and when will progress reports be made?

10. What methods will we use to reproduce copies of the newspaper?

11. If costs are involved for paper or duplicating materials, how will we pay these costs?

12. Will there be advertising? If so, whom will we solicit (in school or out of school)?

13. How will the paper be delivered and to whom?

14. How will we, as a class, evaluate and discuss the experience of producing our own newspaper? Ask such questions as:

    a. What did you enjoy doing the most?

    b. What did you dislike?

    c. What would you change?

    d. What did you learn from this experience?

    e. General comments

REMEMBER — JOURNALISM IS COMMUNICATION! LEARN TO SAY WHAT YOU MEAN AND SAY IT EFFECTIVELY!

Concept

SOURCES OF NEWS
FOR A CLASS NEWSPAPER

The following are important sources for news. Remember, your newspaper index is a content guide.

1. School assemblies
2. Contests
3. Debating and nonathletic teams
4. Dramatics
5. Club
6. Individual class news
7. Sports
8. Hobbies
9. Social news — dances, bake sales, movie night
10. Exchanges with other schools
11. Musical events
12. Concerns from the principal's office or parents
13. Unusual student activities (as a feature article)
14. Teacher, community and parent interviews
15. Grounds and building maintenance — Clean-up campaign
16. Letters to the editor
17. Advice
18. Cartoon and humor
19. Editorial
20. Lunchroom capers
21. Entertaining items
22. News

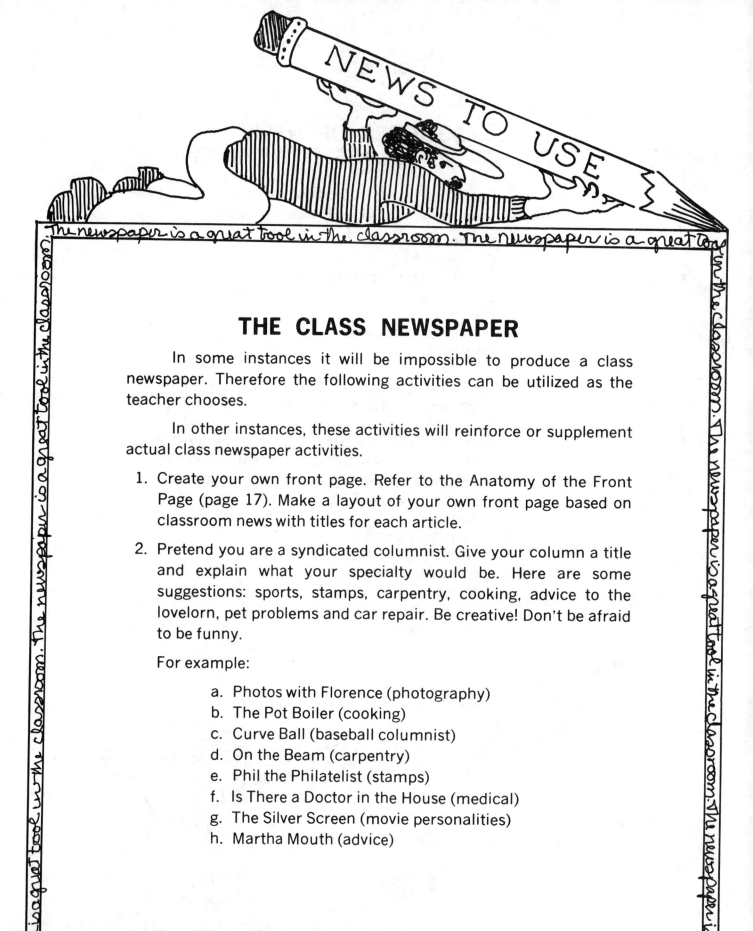

THE CLASS NEWSPAPER

In some instances it will be impossible to produce a class newspaper. Therefore the following activities can be utilized as the teacher chooses.

In other instances, these activities will reinforce or supplement actual class newspaper activities.

1. Create your own front page. Refer to the Anatomy of the Front Page (page 17). Make a layout of your own front page based on classroom news with titles for each article.

2. Pretend you are a syndicated columnist. Give your column a title and explain what your specialty would be. Here are some suggestions: sports, stamps, carpentry, cooking, advice to the lovelorn, pet problems and car repair. Be creative! Don't be afraid to be funny.

   For example:

   - a. Photos with Florence (photography)
   - b. The Pot Boiler (cooking)
   - c. Curve Ball (baseball columnist)
   - d. On the Beam (carpentry)
   - e. Phil the Philatelist (stamps)
   - f. Is There a Doctor in the House (medical)
   - g. The Silver Screen (movie personalities)
   - h. Martha Mouth (advice)

News to Use

3. Here are some important words used in the production of a newspaper. Make your own **word search** puzzle and try to "stump" your friends. See page 54 of this book for the word search scheme.

Headline	Ads
Dateline	By-line
Editor	Classified
Comics	Index
Press	Reporter
News	Cartoonist
Obituary	Photo

4. Write a human interest story which really happened to you, to a friend, or to someone in school. Decide on an incident which you believe classroom newspaper readers would find interesting or funny.

5. Write a straight news story using an historical event as if "You Are There." Be sure to include the 5 W's.

6. Draw a cartoon relating to an important issue at school. It may be humorous or serious.

7. Cover a sports event at school. Use as many colorful adjectives as you can to give your report additional action and excitement. Remember the technique of real sports writers.

News to Use

8. Develop a calendar of class events for the next month. Experiment with different layouts and symbols that represent activities, such as ball and bat, football, movie screen, musical scale, etc.

9. Do a feature column called "Newsy Snacks." Select one food that interests you and tell its history. For example, describe a sandwich and its beginnings with its inventor, The Earl of Sandwich in England.

10. Pretend you are a managing editor of your school newspaper. Your job is to make a production schedule. This includes the stories, names of reporters, and due dates for submitting the material.

REPORTER	ASSIGNMENT	DUE DATE	FINISHED
John L. Green	Baseball		
Sylvia Simon	Lunchroom News		
Leona Marla	Student Council		
Billy Lipsy	Teacher Interviews		
Steve Howard	Editorial		
Mel Barclay	Feature		
Harry Reldan	Artist		

If you wish, use the names of your classmates, your own classroom assignments and the actual due dates of the stories. If your publication date is three weeks from now, on what days will assignments be due? Remember, it takes time to correct (edit) and duplicate (print) the material.

THE EARL OF SANDWICH

News to Use

11. A newspaper should serve the interests of its readers. Design a short questionnaire listing the subjects you propose for your paper. Survey your classmates to determine what kinds of articles they would like to read in the class newspaper. Make a graph indicating the number of people surveyed and what their interests really are.

12. Have a mock press conference. Select a personality who will be the subject of the conference, as in "Meet the Press." This will be a group effort in class. The students must select an issue around which the questions will be asked. The reporters should prepare meaningful questions in advance. Have different reporters write their own interpretations and impressions of the press conference.

13. A newspaper must be accurate — both in its use of facts, as well as in punctuation. The following represents a copy editor's symbols to a writer or typesetter. For example, these symbols mean:

⊄ new paragraph,   ⹀ capitalize

Everybody loves a code! Think of these symbols as a code. Use some of these symbols to correct the following paragraph:

⊄ new paragraph   # insert space
ℓ omit or delete   ⌒ close up
∫ transpose   ∧ insert
∪ join   sp spelling
⹀ capitalize   ⌐ raise
l.c. lower case   ⌐ lower
(/) insert parentheses
ᵛⱽ insert apostrophe or quotes

News to Use

Correct this paragraph using a copy editor's symbols.

Bears Win Home Game

it was hot sticky Thurs. afternoon at the Civic stadium to day when the players ran out on the feild cheered on by there loyal fans simper simon, the star of the teem took adeep bow as the crowd went wild! He through 20 to 30 balls to the catcher as a crowd pleaser. Simons form was better than last season when he tried to get buy with a week pitch arm. Yesterdays win was a victory for Simon, the Bares & his Fans. Good lurck Bears.

WHO AND HOW TO INTERVIEW

Interviewing is one of the most exciting parts of newspaper reporting. It is a type of entertaining writing that requires special preparation — sometimes even more than straight news writing. In addition to research, which all reporters must do, an interviewer must also prepare specific questions.

An interviewer should be pleasant and respectful. Asking good questions that require thoughtful answers is a skill to develop. Recording answers accurately and writing the interview as rapidly as possible are key ingredients to producing a good story.

The Big Activity

Generally, there is a time lag between the moment of the interview and the time when the story is committed to print. This gives the reporter an opportunity to polish and refine his/her article, to reconsider some answers and even to ask the question "Is this really what occurred or what was said?"

The following procedure lists the steps which can be followed for a successful interview:

1. Research information about the person you will interview.

2. Make an appointment and describe the subject to be discussed with the person to be interviewed.

3. Plan questions that require more than "yes" or "no" answers.

4. Be properly prepared with paper, pencil or tape recorder.

5. Both you and the interviewee should stay on the subject.

6. Do not overstay your time. Check your watch.

7. Do not express your opinion. You are there only to ask questions and get answers.

8. Thank the person for his/her time and cooperation.

9. Rewrite your notes immediately while the information is fresh in your mind.

10. Always use good taste and judgment in your reporting. Have your interview reread by your editor or teacher-sponsor.

The Big Activity

PEOPLE TO INTERVIEW — SOME SUGGESTIONS

Many people have a fascinating story to tell. Look around and ask members of your family, school and community. It isn't just the celebrity or important person who has something to share. Be sensitive to the richness of everyone's background. People need only to be asked; most are very pleased to respond. Consider people with unusual backgrounds or occupations — old people, immigrants, workers, professionals, community volunteers and students.

People with Unusual Backgrounds

Older citizens
Artisans (electricians, plumbers, carpenters, chefs, etc.)
Professionals
Volunteers
Business people
Immigrants

Community Service Personnel

Fire
Police
Garbage collectors
Gas or electric meter readers
Telephone line persons
Judges
School board members

School Personnel

Coach
Principal
Teachers
Custodian
Speech therapist
Nurse

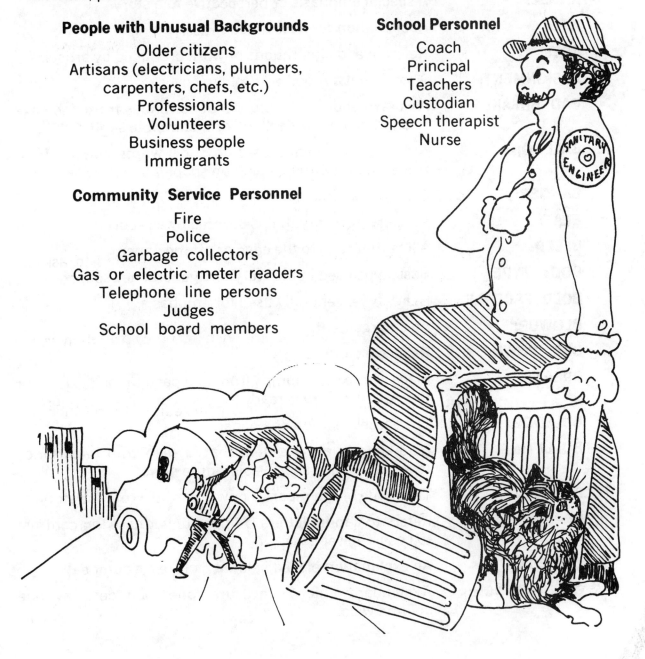

XIV. GLOSSARY OF NEWSPAPER TERMS

This is a general list of definitions. Various disciplines and different geographic areas may use other terms.

AD:	An abbreviation for an advertisement.
ADD:	Additional copy to a story that has already been written.
ADVANCE:	A preliminary story regarding a future event.
AGATE LINE:	A unit for measuring advertising space, one column wide and one-fourteenth of an inch deep.
ALIVE:	Type or copy that is still usable.
A.M.:	Refers to a morning edition.
ANGLE:	A special emphasis or perspective to a story.
A.P.:	Abbreviation for **A**ssociated **P**ress.
ART:	Reference to illustrations or work produced by artists.
ASSIGNMENT:	A story that a reporter is told to cover.
BAD BREAK:	Awkward ending of a story that continues from one page to another with a short line or incomplete sentence.
BALLOON:	A cartoon technique used to show words coming from someone's mouth in a balloon shape.
BANNER:	A large headline.
BEAT:	A regular territory that is covered by a reporter.
BLEED:	A line that runs to the edge or off the paper.
BODY TYPE:	Basic type used in the story and general newspaper.
BOLD FACE/B.F.:	Heavy type, generally used for emphasis.
BLOWUP:	An enlargement.
BOIL DOWN:	Reduce a story.
BREAK:	Place where story jumps from one page to the next, or the time when a story is ready for publication. A story "break."
BULLDOG:	The earliest edition of a paper.
BULLETING:	Reference to a news item that is second in importance to a "flash." It is short, last minute news.
BY-LINE:	The name of the reporter or writer who wrote the story.
CAPS:	Refers to capital letters U.C. or "upper case" in contrast to l.c. or "lower case."
CAPTION:	An explanation placed below a picture—a cutline.
COLUMN INCH:	A standard unit of measure, one inch deep by one column wide.

COPY:	Written or typed material for publication.
COPY DESK:	A special desk where a copy reader sits. The desk is often in a half circle or horseshoe shape.
COPYREADER:	A member of the newspaper staff who edits (corrects) copy. Sometimes he/she writes the headlines.
COPYRIGHT:	An author's legal protection against theft of a written work.
CORRESPONDENT:	An out-of-town or out-of-country reporter.
COVER:	Term used to describe getting all the important facts for a story; for example, the reporter "covered" the story.
CUB:	A new, generally young reporter.
CUT:	To reduce the length of a story. Also an illustration or a photograph.
CUTLINE:	A few lines of written information explaining the picture.
DATELINE:	A dateline is not a date. It is the beginning line of the story stating **where** the event took place.
DEAD:	Story material that is usually set in type that is no longer usable.
DEADLINE:	Final time when copy for a newspaper edition is due or may be accepted.
DISPLAY TYPE:	Larger than normal body type, used for headlines and ads.
DRAGON'S BLOOD:	An etching powder which is red, dry and resinous, used in the photoengraving process.
DUMMY:	A layout of a newspaper page that shows the arrangement of headlines, stories and pictures.
EAR:	Information placed on either side of the front page, usually in a box.
EDITORIALIZE:	To express an opinion in a newspaper article. Editorials appear on the editorial page.
EXCLUSIVE:	A special story given to only one reporter and published in only one newspaper.
FACE:	The characteristic style of a typeface such as Italic; also refers to a printing surface of a piece of type that touches the paper.
FEATURE:	A story that is entertaining and not strictly news.
FILLER:	A story with little news value, used to fill up part of a column.
FLAG:	Title of the newspaper appearing on the front page.

FLASH:	The first brief news announcement of an important story.
FOLLOW-UP:	A story that provides additional information to one printed earlier.
FONT:	A complete collection (A through Z) of a typeface's style and size.
FOURTH ESTATE:	Traditional term for the press.
FYI:	An abbreviation for, **F**or **Y**our **I**nformation.
GALLEY PROOF:	A proof (a kind of reproduction) of type before it is printed on newspaper pages.
HEADLINE OR BANNER:	A large heading which runs across the width of the front page or most of it.
HOLD:	A shortened phrase for "hold for release."
HOLE:	Vacancy on a page to be filled.
INDEX:	The alphabetical list and numbered location of each section of the paper which appears on the front page.
INTERVIEW:	A story based on a question and answer session generally conducted by the reporter.
JUMP LINE:	Tells the page number on which the story is continued.
JUSTIFY:	To space out a line of type to full margin; to create an even margin on both sides.
KILL:	To remove part or all of copy from a news story.
l.c.:	An abbreviation for lower case, in contrast to U.C. for capitals.
LEAD:	The first few lines of a news story which contain the kernel of the story, or the five W's: **W**ho, **W**hat, **W**here, **W**hen, **W**hy.
LEAD STORY:	The story that explains the headline, the most important story on the front page.
MASTHEAD:	Information that generally appears on top of the editorial page providing the name of the paper, ownership, place of publication, subscription rates, etc.
MORGUE:	A reference library in a newspaper where old stories, photographs, etc., are stored.
OBIT:	Abbreviation for obituary.
PAD:	To make a story longer by using unnecessary words.
P.M.:	Afternoon edition of a newspaper.
PROOF:	A reproduction of a page of type or art for the purpose of making corrections.

PUT TO BED: A term describing that an edition has been typeset and is ready to be printed.

PROOFREADER: Person who reads and corrects proof pages or stories.

RELEASE DATE: Specific date that identifies when a story will appear in a newspaper.

REWRITE: To write a story provided by a "legman" (a person who gets the facts); also to revise a story to make it better.

R.O.P.: Run-of-paper news and advertising which appears in any convenient spot in a newspaper.

RULE: A metal strip that prints as a line to separate or cut off columns.

SPOT NEWS: Unexpected, fresh news.

SPREAD: A big and important layout, as in "a full-page spread."

STET: "Let it stand," a term used by proofreaders to disregard the correction that was made.

STYLE BOOK: A special book for a newspaper's reporters, editors and printers that gives directions and rules for a specific typographical style.

SUBHEAD: Headings used throughout a story to break the solid look of a column. Subheads are generally in bold type.

SYNDICATE: An organization that sells articles to newspaper for simultaneous publication.

TABLOID: A smaller newspaper (11" x 15"), usually five columns wide.

THIRTY: The end of a story shown as # # # or -30-.

TYPO: A shortened word for typographical error.

UPI: Abbreviation for United Press International.

UPPER CASE: Capital letters or U.C.

WIDOW: A short word or part of a word that stands alone on a line at the end of a paragraph.

WIRE SERVICE: News services which supply national and international news, such as Associated Press (A.P.), United Press International (UPI), Reuters, New York Times, etc.

WIREPHOTO: A photo transmitted by telephone or telegraph.

WRAP UP: When all copy is in the composing room, when an edition is "wrapped up", a story is "wrapped up" or when all the facts are in.